ONE TO TEN

FINDING YOUR WAY
FROM STARTUP TO SCALEUP

ONE
TO
TEN

RAGS GUPTA

LIONCREST
PUBLISHING

ONE TO TEN
Finding Your Way from Startup to Scaleup

ISBN   978-1-5445-2285-2 *Hardcover*
        978-1-5445-2286-9 *Paperback*
        978-1-5445-2283-8 *Ebook*

*To startup founders everywhere. Thank you for grinding
away to bring us a better future, for risking it all to make
a dent in the universe. You inspire me every day.*

And to Babes, Babu, and Mishti. You are my dream come true.

CONTENTS

INTRODUCTION

"The first $10 million is the hardest."

—JASON CALACANIS

Here's what they don't tell you about going from Zero to One: that's the easy part.

Most startup tech founders create *something* out of nothing, raise their first institutional rounds, convince some early adopters to pay for their product. They grow the kernel of what could become a real business.

Then they hit a wall.

They struggle to progress past customer pilots. To transcend founder-led sales. To go from a scrappy group pitching in to build out an executive team and a well-functioning organization. To find the right role for each founder. To execute their first reorganization. And, especially, to get to $10 million in revenue.

The going gets messy during the One-to-Ten phase, that

awkward adolescence when a startup scales beyond its first customers, its early team, its first million in revenue.

The result? Bridge rounds. Employee attrition. Scathing Glassdoor reviews. Revenue misses. Executive team shake-ups. Founder breakups. Dilution. "Landing the plane" via an acquihire. Or worse, perishing in the startup valley of death.

Any of this sound familiar to you?

I, for one, have seen this movie play out many times during my twenty-odd years in tech. And yet, it's a phase rarely discussed in the startup world. Plenty is written about finding product–market fit or navigating "blitz-scaled hypergrowth," but the transition phase is rarely talked about.[1] I'm here to change that. This book will help you through each step of the One-to-Ten phase.

What do I mean by One to Ten? Let's first abstract the startup journey into three phases. Take a look at the following chart for a basic understanding of each phase.

---

1   Three notable exceptions that cover this phase well include *The Messy Middle* by Scott Belsky, *High Growth Handbook* by Elad Gil, and *First Round Review*.

	0 to 1	1 to 10	10 to X
Theme	• Innovation • Product Market Fit	• Transition • Go-to-Market Fit	• Acceleration • Build Flywheel
Product	• Prototypes, Alphas • Missing Table Stakes	• Feature Complete • Production/GA	• Multiple Products • Build Moat
Go to Market	• Founder-led Sales • Pilots/Beta Customers • Define ICP, Beachhead Markets	• Hire Go-to-Market Team • Non-founder Sales • Penetrate Beachhead Markets	• Multiple Segments • Multiple Sales Motions • International
Human Capital	• Utility Players • Key Functions Outsourced • Amorphuous Roles	• First Exec team • Build Key Functions • Org Design	• Teams of Teams • Repeatable Hiring • Org Scaling
Funding	• Pre-seed/Seed	• Seed – Series A – Series B	• Series B+

YOU ARE HERE

ZERO TO ONE: INNOVATION

In the beginning, you leverage your entrepreneurial insight to create something that other people want. This phase, all about finding product–market fit, involves lab work, prototypes and alpha products, maybe your initial 1.0 product. You and your co-founders are landing your first customers, whether they're called pilots, beta users, or design partners. This stage is all about innovation, about doing things that don't scale.

ONE TO TEN: TRANSITION

Going from One to Ten requires different muscle than what got you from Zero to One. It requires transitions that you've likely never encountered before, much less imagined the right strategy for. You'll see changes from shipping alpha and beta versions to general availability, from doing things that don't scale to putting in processes and protocols to reliably service multiple customers, from founder selling to productive reps who can sell without you. You'll build out your management team and key functions during this stage, which itself will be a major transition for you and your early employees.

TEN TO X: ACCELERATION

Once you've proven repeatability of sales and product, this phase is about accelerating growth and finding new S curves of growth, building on the foundation you have in place. This may involve new products, new ways of selling, new markets, and new teams.

Where are you on your journey? This book is to help founders find their way during the One-to-Ten transition phase, when startups grow into scaleups. Take a few recent examples of founders currently finding their way.

Jonathan Tushman and Sonci Honnoll are founders of Quala.io, a next-gen customer success platform based in Boston. Having founded Quala in 2018, Jonathan and Sonci have successfully navigated the Zero-to-One phase with the first version of their platform, their first couple dozen customers, and a top-notch team comprising product, sales, growth, and engineering. But they know that, to get to the next level, they'll need to deliver the table-stakes features expected by their target market, while proving that their new revenue team can sell without them.

"I've helped land every pharma and biotech deal that we've done so far. We need to figure out how to scale beyond just me selling." That's Abhishek Jha (a.k.a. AJ), founder/CEO of Elucidata, a venture capital (VC)-backed bioinformatics data platform. AJ faces the classic scaling problem of going beyond founder selling. Elucidata needs to build a repeatable sales machine to get to Ten.

"We need to hire a VP of ops. Right now, my co-founder Brent is waking up at five a.m. every day to deal with our site deployments…but the people we're considering would be the most senior in our company and it makes us nervous!" Damon Henry, co-founder and CEO of Asylon, a drone platform startup providing aerial security to customers such as FedEx and Ford, told me this in a recent conversation. Their drone-in-a-box systems are flying hundreds of missions each month across a number of sites. Damon needs to scale his organization to take Asylon to the next level.

To get to Ten, every business-to-business (B2B) startup needs to nail product readiness, to build a repeatable sales machine, and to scale their human capital. These form a three-legged stool with each leg needing to be in harmony with the other two. For example, you may achieve product readiness and have a great team built out but you'll flounder without repeatable sales. Another common failure mode is to prematurely scale your org way ahead of product maturity. This book covers the common mistakes to avoid, mental models, and best practices to lay the foundation for growth.

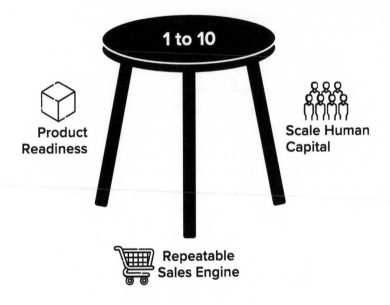

Product Readiness

Scale Human Capital

Repeatable Sales Engine

Once you do get to Ten, the sky's the limit. As Jason Lemkin, founder of Echosign and SaaS guru investor, put it, "If you can get to $10 million in revenue, you can get to a thousand million."

Having spent twenty-plus years operating and investing in VC-backed startups and scaleups, I've seen a lot. The outcomes range from bankruptcy (Rollup Media) to a zombie (Live365) to an acquisition (Videoplaza) to an IPO (Brightcove). And those are just the companies I've operated.[2] I've also invested in, advised, or mentored countless other startups over the years.[3]

Unsuccessful startups are all alike; every successful startup is successful in its own way.[4]

---

2   It's too early to know the outcome at Humatics where I was COO. At the time of writing, they'd completed their Series B.

3   Visit my profiles on AngelList or Crunchbase for more detail on my portfolio.

4   With apologies to Tolstoy!

And now, a word from my lawyer:[5] startup advice is highly context-specific. The advice you get during the Zero-to-One phase may be terrible advice for the One-to-Ten phase. And vice versa. Every founder and company has their unique context, and you are no different. That said, while the settings and characters differ, the plotlines often follow similar arcs. So, this book articulates principles and frameworks to navigate growing pains common to startups. It's geared toward first-time technical or product-centric entrepreneurs operating B2B startups with an emphasis on top-down sales since there's so much written about bottom-up, product-led models.

It's organized around the three legs of the stool.

Part 1 on Product Readiness provides mental models and case studies to determine if your product is ready for scale. I'll also offer tips for avoiding scaling prematurely, especially relevant for deep tech ventures but applicable to software startups too.

Part 2 on Repeatable Sales offers best practices in getting your sales machine humming. We'll start with honing your sales motion and cover everything from running great meetings to negotiating and closing deals to building out your go-to-market team.

Part 3 on Scaling Human Capital focuses on the people at your startup. It gives you tools to operate and scale your company, from putting a strategic plan together to developing an operating cadence to building out the organization, concluding with advice on how to scale yourself.

---

5   Actually, it's just me giving the obligatory caveat!

Each part is written to stand alone, so feel free to skip to the parts that are most relevant to you. But the book works as a complete experience if you're on the cusp of the One-to-Ten journey.

Most startups fail to scale due to internal factors that were under their control. That's why I wrote this book. If this book helps you close just one more deal or avoid a costly hiring mistake, or even just gives you more confidence in handling your startup's growing pains, it will have been worth it for us both. And if it doesn't, I'd love to hear from you to see about giving your money back.

Ready?

Let's do this.

PART 1

PRODUCT READINESS

In the fall of 2012 I made my first customer visit at Videoplaza[6] at M6, the second-largest French broadcaster, and one of our top accounts. I'd expected the meeting to be mainly relationship building, a courtesy visit.

Instead, they laid into me. What I expected to be a pleasant meet and greet became a venting session about the status of our road map and, especially, the poor state of our reporting. We were the system of record for their digital video advertising and our slow, buggy reporting was unacceptable. I scrambled to apologize and promised to look into their issues.

Fast-forward a few hours. I'm in the office of our French VC dialed into a board call where our chief technology officer proudly touts the velocity of the engineering team and how their various projects were on track. Huh?

It was a massive disconnect. Our platform wasn't ready to scale. Worse, we had embarked on a project that, in hindsight, kneecapped our growth and destroyed company value. It was a dumpster fire. The original sins were many but came down to the wrong architecture choice and ineffective product management.

Architecturally, the team had decided to build on Hadoop, a promising but immature platform. I kept hearing about how we were one of the biggest Hadoop instances in the world. That's great, except we didn't have the resources to support it while working on other features. We had dug ourselves into a massive hole and there was little choice but to keep digging.

---

6   Videoplaza was a digital video ad monetization platform started in Stockholm. I first joined as an independent board member and, later, as chief commercial officer.

The worst part? The team had decided to build real-time reporting first, sequencing historical reporting for later. But here's the rub: customers didn't actually **care** about real-time reporting. It was a nice-to-have, glitzy feature, but not to be used for decision-making. What they really needed was bulletproof, lightning-fast historical reporting.

I remember my utter dismay when I finally grokked the disconnect. It was at our 2013 annual sales kickoff meeting when a sales exec took me aside and filled me in. We'd been tap-dancing with customers to buy our team time only to deliver a product that customers didn't need. There was a massive gap in understanding between the customers' requirements and what engineering delivered. I kick myself still, wondering how I could have more quickly understood and flagged this even while I was on the board. Sigh.

We never did nail reporting. It was a sore spot for everyone. The topic lingered at every customer QBR[7] and took away from our myriad other accomplishments. Engineers didn't want to work on the product, riddled with technical debt, that was considered table stakes by customers. The most insidious part was the lack of confidence that my field sales team then had in our platform, eventually leading to lower close rates and higher churn. And then there was the distraction. So much time was spent unwinding decisions that had been made, firefighting, or doing manual work-arounds—time that could have been spent developing new features or going on offense into new markets and customer segments.

Videoplaza never got to Ten. We had dozens of customers, a stel-

---

7 Quarterly business review.

lar team, a special culture, and triple-digit percentage growth, but we never did break the $10 million revenue barrier. I'm convinced that our lack of product readiness played a big role in this.

It wasn't all bad news. We'd built a decision engine using neural networks that was ahead of its time. Even better, we had enough traction to take advantage of market consolidation in video ad tech and sell the business at a strategic valuation.[8] But I'll always wonder how big we could have grown Videoplaza had we not had the reporting millstone around our neck.

Your product underpins your company's foundation. Build on a shaky foundation, or on the wrong site for the wrong customer, and you'll spend so much energy on patching and repairing that you'll lose the opportunity to go on offense. Even worse, you'll burn valuable capital scaling prematurely while fighting fires along the way.

Product Readiness doesn't just mean the technology, however. The Product Readiness "formula" comprises three components:

$$\text{Product Readiness} = \text{Customer Value} \times \text{Value Capture} \times \text{Scalability}^9$$

Customer Value involves defining *what* you're selling, identifying *to whom* you're selling, understanding *why* they buy, and quantifying *how much* value they realize. The quest for Product Readiness requires horizontal technology startups to

---

8   Greater than 10x revenue multiple, all cash, which was rich in 2014 for a subscale European enterprise startup!

9   I define Product–Market fit to be the first two variables: Customer Value and Value Capture. But you need Scalability to achieve Product Readiness and get to Ten and beyond.

choose beachhead markets and deep tech startups to escape pilot purgatory. We'll cover this in Chapters 1 and 2.

Value Capture, Chapter 3's topic, requires committing to a business model and pricing to capture a fair share of the value you're creating. You won't be ready to scale if you don't have this nailed down.

Scalability doesn't just involve your core technology. It includes other, often overlooked aspects key to scaling such as documentation, support, and product marketing, addressed in Chapter 4.

Lastly, even if you have elements of each formula in place, you will need to make the important call of declaring your product ready, of shipping to production, which I'll cover in Chapter 5.

CHAPTER 1

◈

VALIDATE YOUR VALUE PROPOSITION

November 2, 2020. The *Wall Street Journal* broke the news that Walmart was terminating its yearslong relationship with Bossa Nova Robotics,[10] a robotics startup out of Carnegie Mellon. Even worse for Bossa Nova, the coverage reported that the retailer had come up with simpler, more cost-effective solutions to the problem of stocking shelves using human workers instead, putting Bossa Nova's entire value proposition into question. Bossa Nova, with its robots in hundreds of Walmart stores, had clearly found their way from One to Ten and beyond. And yet, the value proposition with their largest customer didn't add up or had changed with the pandemic.[11]

It's not enough for customers to be interested or even willing to pay to evaluate your product. They must be able to achieve business value and continue to do so over time. It's easy for

---

10   Sarah Nassauer, "Walmart Scraps Plan to Have Robots Scan Shelves," *Wall Street Journal*, November 2, 2020, https://www.wsj.com/articles/walmart-shelves-plan-to-have-robots-scan-shelves-11604345341.

11   Soon after, Bossa Nova laid off 50 percent of their workforce. Having spoken to their impressive founder, Sarjoun Skaff, in the past, I am betting that they will rebound in due course.

early-stage startups to get caught up in the excitement of winning blue-chip logo pilot customers only to realize they actually didn't deliver value.

You should be able to crisply articulate and quantify the value your customers derive from your product.

How do you go about this? Develop a comprehensive understanding of the who, what, why, and how of your customers' journey. Start with the basics to lay the right foundation for growth.

IDEAL CUSTOMER PROFILE (ICP)

While you may have defined buyer personas and the ideal customer profile during the Zero-to-One phase, consider if your personas and ICP will change during this next stage of growth. This is often the case where you may have tested your minimum viable product with other startups or early adopters but, to get to $10 million in revenue and beyond, you'll need to target a different type of buyer.

TABLE STAKES

Do you have the table stakes features for your ICP? Startups often overlook these, especially when they've been focusing on breakthrough innovation during the Zero-to-One phase. But even the most innovative product may fail to convert leads if it lacks basic features that the buyer considers to be standard. Missing table stakes features reduce your addressable market and extend sales cycles and are tightly connected to your ICP. What may be nice to have for one segment will be a must-have for another segment. Tune your road map to incorporate table stakes features for new ICPs.

CUSTOMER ENGAGEMENT

Robust customer engagement is a leading indicator that you're driving value, especially repeat buying. These are the customers who want more from your team, who heavily use your products and come back for more. These customers, especially the repeat buyers, should heavily inform your ICP.

Additionally, explicit customer sentiment will tell you where your company should go during this critical growth period. You can measure customer sentiment in both qualitative and quantitative ways. Rahul Vohra, founder of Superhuman, surveys his customers with a simple question, "How would you feel if you could no longer use Superhuman?" with the answer choices being Very Disappointed, Somewhat Disappointed, and Not Disappointed.[12]

The magic threshold is 40 percent. *If more than 40 percent of the users you poll would be very disappointed, you have product–market fit. Experts stipulate that you need at least forty responses from those who have already tried your product to get direction-ally correct results.* Of course, this method will be easy for some and much harder for B2B companies with smaller customer bases. The habit of tracking customer sentiment, and tying it to your company's goals and behaviors, however, is critical. Find a way that makes sense for your company and make sure you stick to it, particularly as your base grows.

Sometimes you'll notice that what customers say doesn't align with the data your team has. This is normal, but it also presents a problem as you try to grow. To mitigate the risks, find a way

---

12   Rahul Vohra, "How Superhuman Built an Engine to Find Product/Market
      Fit," First Round Review, accessed June 13, 2021, https://firstround.com/review/
      how-superhuman-built-an-engine-to-find-product-market-fit.

to track implicit customer behavior as well. Observe your customers using your product in situ. Do their actions back up their feedback? Is the product being used more or less than expected? Customers may say good things about your product, but be sure that their actions back this up. You could have your robot system deployed with good feedback only to learn that it's gathering dust in the corner and not being used. The last thing you want is to make decisions based on feedback from people who aren't using your product at all, so be diligent about this data.

Other times, the customers will chase you. They won't take no for an answer. They qualify you back in. This is market pull, and an indication that you've identified a problem that the market desperately needs solved. This happened with one of our largest customers at one of my companies. They had a large pilot with a notoriously slow-moving customer that was used to having vendors jumping through hoops for their business. It was getting toward the end of the pilot and they still didn't know whether the customer would proceed further. So, the CEO let the customer executive know that they might need to stand the team down to focus on other verticals. That got a strong reaction. The customer opened up and made it crystal clear that the company wasn't to walk. This is market pull.

What do these heuristics have in common? Customer engagement. Engagement can manifest itself in disappointment and even anger. This isn't so bad! It means they care! Customer apathy is much, much worse. In fact, watch out for red herrings in your quest to validate product–market fit.

Too often, we hear what we want to hear. We take praise as a sign that we're on the right path rather than probing further to deeply understand the customer's problem, where it ranks on their list of priorities, and how our solution really stacks up. Then we are surprised when the customer doesn't buy.

Beware vanity metrics—key performance indicators (KPIs) that make you feel good but don't actually tie to business value for the customer. During the COVID-19 pandemic, I advised the PathCheck Foundation, an all-volunteer MIT Media Lab spin-out led by the genius polymath Ramesh Raskar and dedicated to privacy-preserving digital pandemic response technology. It was amazing to see the caliber of talent that the project attracted. Programmers, former CEOs, DC policy wonks, lawyers—all signed up to help the cause. We would keep track of the number of volunteers and trumpet it in our communications. There was just one problem: the states and countries we were pitching didn't care. Would you trust mission-critical pandemic technology to an all-volunteer organization? In hindsight, the number of volunteers was a vanity metric that didn't actually reflect the value that PathCheck was delivering to its users.

UNDERSTAND WHY CUSTOMERS BUY

Do you know why your customers buy your product? This is the heart of your value proposition. It's not just about your product's features. Buyers justify purchases along three vectors:

1. *Direct cost savings.* Robotics systems are a good example here. They are predominantly valued based on labor savings with other benefits being important but not driving the sale. These tend to be return on investment (ROI)-driven transactions with payback period being a key buyer metric.
2. *Revenue increase.* You're in a great place if your product can increase customer revenues. Adtech platforms are a good example of this category, as are platforms like Gong

or Chorus that focus on sales productivity. Customers justify purchasing these platforms based on the expected revenue increase. Sometimes your product enables the customer to create a new business line, in which case you will help them build the business case.

3. *Future-proofing "insurance."* These are frequently new platforms that enable workflow transformation such as Slack or Airtable. Buyers of future-proofing products recognize that they may need to fundamentally alter their business processes and workflows and that your product may allow them to do so should the world change. These sales may include value calculators to help justify the investment, but they are inherently harder to calculate.

The categories above aren't mutually exclusive. At Videoplaza, we frequently competed against DoubleClick, the dominant ad platform owned by Google. On the face of it, our value proposition was all about helping publishers maximize their digital video advertising revenues. We developed ROI calculators and case studies around the incremental revenue to be earned by switching to us.

But we also realized that our customers were hiring us for something else. We were an insurance policy. They didn't want their data and revenues flowing through Google, nor did they want to have their competitor controlling the road map of mission-critical technology. This was especially resonant in Europe with its skepticism of the big American digital giants. We adapted our pitch accordingly and stressed our European roots and commitment to services—a message that landed well at the C-suite.

Show proof of cost savings or revenue increase when selling against those vectors.

But what about when selling a future-proofing platform? In these cases, *lead the customer to the "aha" moment as early as possible.*

That's what the successful product-led growth (PLG) companies do, by driving product usage so users can see for themselves. But this need not be limited to PLG companies.

In the early days of Brightcove, creating and publishing streaming video players was a cumbersome, expensive process requiring a large in-house team or expensive outsourced shops. We'd articulate our vision for a cloud-based video publishing platform and then, in front of their eyes, would create a Flash video player in their brand with dummy content and launch the player during the meeting itself. The demos were jaw-dropping. Customers couldn't believe what they saw.

They had an inkling that streaming could be a transformative business opportunity (or threat) and knew they'd need to be future-proofed when that day came. Our job was then to convince them that Brightcove would be the platform partner for them during this transition. We would go on to justify the investment in our platform based on reducing streaming and publishing costs and increasing digital video revenues, but we started with the vision of a platform to usher in their transition to digital as the entry point.

Understanding your customers and why they buy underpins product readiness. Don't work on hardening the product or reducing technical debt until you've established this foundation.

COMMIT TO A BEACHHEAD MARKET

Entrepreneurship starts with insight based on market, technology, or, ideally, both. Market-based insights start with what the market needs and then determine the technologies to bring to bear to fill the need. Rylan Hamilton and Jerome Dubois, the founders of 6 River Systems, are a perfect example of entrepreneurs launching based on both market and technology insights.

Having worked at Kiva Systems and then Amazon after its acquisition, they noted how the robotic warehouse system that had been developed at Kiva could benefit a new swath of the market if it were cheaper and more flexible. Not every customer could afford the tens of millions of dollars needed to build a Kiva warehouse from the ground up. There was also the little detail that Amazon was going to exclusively use the Kiva technology for its own fulfillment centers rather than continue to sell to others.

There was a clear market gap. In addition, they knew that the cost of robotic systems would decrease over time. These insights drove the founding of 6 River Systems. The rest is history. 6 River Systems sold to Shopify for $450 million in September 2019, three and a half years after their $6 million Series A round.[13]

In contrast to market insights, technology insights start with the invention of new technologies and a discovery process to determine the best applications. This is inevitably a more meandering, less capital-efficient path. Like the scientific method, customer discovery involves forming hypotheses and trying to disprove them. It's particularly challenging in that you may

---

13   A large part of the transaction was in Shopify stock, which is up more than 3x since the acquisition closed, making the price well north of $450 million if the stock were held by the sellers.

have a few customers in a vertical, convincing you that you've attained product–market fit, whereas your value proposition still hasn't been proven out. The shorter the feedback loop, the faster you determine if you're driving customer value. Ultimately the best signal is if these customers grow their business with you over time. More on this later.

Choose one, max two, beachhead markets, especially when operating in supply-constrained markets.

Most deep tech startups are fortunate to operate in a supply-constrained market. There is literally more demand than you can supply. Take autonomous vehicles. Even before the COVID-19 pandemic, there was essentially limitless demand for safe, reasonably priced robotaxis. Post-pandemic, that demand has ballooned to encompass delivery vehicles that can safely deliver goods to consumers in a contactless manner.

The problem is on the supply side. The technology isn't mature enough to safely operate at scale, to handle the numerous corner cases that may arise, to have the uptime and speed that can match human drivers. There are billions of dollars being invested into companies trying to solve these problems. Their challenge is to marshal their resources despite the strong market pull.

The demand will go to your head. You'll risk biting off more than you can chew. It may be that there are multiple applications for your technology that can each deliver a killer value proposition. You may have explored these in parallel during the Zero-to-One phase, placing multiple small bets across several fields. You may well have a broad, horizontal technology with multiple applications across verticals. Your challenge then is to identify and commit to your first beachhead market, the one that has customers with such "hair on fire" problems that they pull you in despite the rough edges.

You will need multiple customers in each market to prove repeatability and unlock your next round of funding. Series A or B VCs won't fund startups with one customer across a number of segments and applications. Evaluation criteria should include how urgent the problem is for that set of customers, their willingness to pay, the competitive landscape, the size of the market, and, importantly, how good a fit your technology is for the application. Put simply, are you trying to hammer a square peg into a round hole?

Choosing your beachhead market(s) will be one of your most important strategic decisions during the One-to-Ten stage. Do you have the conviction to make this call?

If yes, great. Put other opportunities on the back burner so you can focus on the beachhead. If not, put this book down and keep experimenting until you can make the call (or you're out of runway). Ensure that you are systematically testing hypotheses with as short a feedback loop as possible.

ARTICULATE CUSTOMER VALUE

"We had one slide that did all our selling."

Meet Amy Villeneuve, former President and COO of Kiva Systems. Kiva was a pioneer in warehouse automation founded by visionary Mick Mountz in 2003. Where, previously, humans traversed a warehouse to pick the right products to fulfill an order, the Kiva robotic system ingeniously flipped the model and brought the warehouse to the humans.

Kiva grew revenue into the low tens of millions until a combination of factors caused growth to plateau in 2010. Mick and Kiva's primary investor recruited Amy and the rest is history. Within two years, she had turbocharged revenue and gotten it to profitability, culminating in its sale to Amazon in 2012 for $777 million. It was a steal for Amazon.[14] They went on to form Amazon Robotics with the acquisition and have since rolled out hundreds of thousands of robots based on the Kiva platform that have enabled Amazon to scale their fulfillment centers.

Amy refers to a slide that plotted a large customer's usage of Kiva from the three prior years. "It showed customers buying more over time. They were voting with their dollars and so of course that meant they were realizing value."

Can you make such a slide? If so, proceed to Chapter 3, where I address how to capture your fair share of value. If you're still in customer pilots, and have yet to validate your value proposition, read on.

---

14 Pitchbook's take: "The purchase of Whole Foods will no doubt go down as one of Amazon's most significant acquisitions of this decade—and deservedly so. It was a savvy move, one that put the wider retail industry on notice. But Amazon's deal for Kiva Systems, while perhaps lesser-known, remains the more transformative one, radically changing how the ecommerce giant fulfills millions of orders and potentially saving the company, by some estimates, up to $2.5 billion…The day that Amazon announced the acquisition of Kiva, its stock closed at $185.52 per share…As Amazon further automates its sprawling global supply chain, its acquisition of Kiva six years ago is arguably the deal that's done the most to make that automation happen." Adam Putz, "M&A flashback: Amazon announces $775M Kiva Systems acquisition," Pitchbook, March 19, 2018, https://pitchbook.com/news/articles/ma-flashback-amazon-announces-775m-kiva-systems-acquisition.

CHAPTER 2

ESCAPE PILOT
PURGATORY

I know a founder of a cleantech startup, we'll call it CleanAir-
Co.[15] Over a decade into his journey, he has managed to get
CleanAirCo past Ten. But it has been a slog. There were many
times along the way when it was touch-and-go. CleanAirCo
was founded on a breakthrough idea stemming from academic
research to use nature to not just clean waste but generate positive externalities in the process. After their first couple of years
of proving the technology in the lab and exploring the value
proposition across applications, they landed on the vertical best
suited for the technology.

Three years after founding, CleanAirCo announced their first
pilot customer, a high-profile logo in their target vertical. They
set about making it work and, after several quarters and lots of
blood, sweat, and tears, they were able to exceed the customer's ROI expectations. Alas, the customer still wouldn't move
forward, citing larger priorities and a changed context. What's

---

15 The details have been obfuscated but this is a true story.

worse, in the insular vertical in question, word spread that Clea-nAirCo's initial pilot customer wasn't moving forward, giving pause to their other prospects.

CleanAirCo was in pilot purgatory.

WHAT IS PILOT PURGATORY?

How could one fall into pilot purgatory and what should be done about it? Pilots are implementations of your product to validate business value. They are different from proofs of concept, which demonstrate the viability of the technology. Pilot purgatory is that dreaded place where you are neither here nor there. You show enough promise for the customer to stay engaged but don't prove enough value for the customer to proceed to production.

The best way to escape pilot purgatory is to avoid it in the first place. Since you are proving your value proposition during a pilot, do not do pilots without defined, quantitative success criteria that you have confidence in hitting. Seek pilot customers with the right motivation, resources, and engagement. The less mature and harder tech your product, the higher the stakes in picking the right pilot customers. If you have a SaaS product selling $12,000 per year subscriptions, you can afford to swing and miss with your early customers; you'll have many more shots on goal. Contrast that with a deep tech robotics startup doing a first-of-its-kind implementation with an industry bellwether where nailing the pilot could be existential.

Ensure that you've created a road map for rollout post-pilot. Ideally, you should have an agreement to proceed if certain benchmarks are hit. At minimum, this should be an understanding of the productization process. In CleanAirCo's case, their customer had no obligation to purchase at that site despite CleanAirCo exceeding their ROI expectations. Luckily for CleanAirCo, they were able to have their champion at the customer personally vouch for CleanAirCo's technology and business case to CleanAirCo's other prospects, which unblocked their next few customers. They were back in the game despite having a couple of lost quarters. They found their way from One to Ten and are going strong in 2021. But it was a bumpy ride, to say the least. In hindsight, given the stakes of a capital-intensive first-of-a-kind deployment, CleanAirCo's founder would have insisted on a clause requiring the customer to purchase should their KPIs be met.

Last, create a value case or worksheet. This documents the assumptions behind the value that the customer can achieve, both quantitative and qualitative. Essentially, this is the thesis behind your working together and will be the North Star for the relationship.

ADDRESS COMMON PILOT PURGATORY MODALITIES

While every context is different, there are a few common failure modes underpinning pilots that end up in purgatory.

The performance gap/too many edge cases.

The performance gap is the delta between what your product currently delivers and what's acceptable to roll out in production. System uptime is a common metric, but it could also be productivity KPIs like picks per hour, battery life, or time to perform a task. Let's take uptime. Ninety-nine percent availability may sound great but in practice it means 7.3 hours a month that your system is down. Edge cases reduce uptime and tend to drive the performance gap. They can require too much human intervention or more time to train machine learning models. All of this means a longer time to value for the customer. In these instances, you have a few options:

- **Constrain, constrain, constrain.** The more constrained the problem, the fewer edge cases and higher uptime. Even when you think it's way too constrained, it probably isn't. You will need to carefully balance constraints with customer value. Constrain too much and you'll erode your value proposition. Strike this balance by creating a short feedback loop with the customer and your product and engineering team to test any potential constraints that you impose on the system against the customer's expectation of value.
- **Put humans in the loop.** As technical entrepreneurs, it's tempting to automate everything that can be automated. However, strategically using humans in collaboration with machines will let you have the best of both worlds. Take Plus One Robotics: their machine vision software is used by their customers' robots for package picking operations. The robots operate autonomously and only flag themselves to a remote human teleoperator when edge cases arise. A teleoperator can oversee multiple robots remotely, making the economics attractive.
- **Use partners.** Partners can develop custom integrations on top of your product to solve specific use cases for their customers. The MiR material handling platform, now owned by Teradyne, is a good example of this. Their partners design various fixtures for MiR robots based on the use case at hand, enabling MiR to constrain their problem space and focus on the base platform instead of building for their customers' myriad use cases.

Poorly qualified pilots.

We've all signed on to do pilots where the success criteria were never well defined or became murkier over time. Many startups take on pilots that are glorified proofs of concept, often selling to the innovation teams of large enterprises. These exercises can prove a technology fit, but don't actually uncover the value necessary to scale customer base. In these cases:

- **Level set expectations and stop further work until the success criteria and a value exercise are defined.** Call a summit where each party can level set on what's been learned so far and where to take it. These can be productive ways to draw a line under the past and work out a mutual plan to align on success criteria and a value discovery exercise.
- **Push back when the goalposts change.** Use the value hypothesis that you have in place to convincingly push back on a customer that's changing the goalposts. Maybe you've already demonstrated the eighteen-month payback period that they sought and they're now pushing for fourteen months. Push back or get something in return.
- **Productize your pilots.** If customers insist on trying your product out in their own environment, fix as many variables as you can. Standardizing entitlements and constraining the number and types of integrations can shorten this part of the cycle. For instance, you might put together an eval kit spelling out X hours of remote support. The customer then knows they need to fully leverage your team's time, or they'll have to pay for more.

Imbalanced resourcing and disengaged customers.

Aligning resources and ensuring the right engagement with

the customer are critical for successful pilots. When this isn't in place, you can expect the following scenarios:

- **Bringing a knife to a gunfight.** Ensure that you've set yourself up for success in terms of resources and focus. That was another lesson learned by CleanAirCo. They struggled on the services and operations side in their first large deployments due to an inexperienced team. As the founder said, "Our technology worked. We just didn't staff the project the right way. Instead of a bright, scrappy but green team, we really needed more experienced hands on the project. We got there in the end, but it cost us time, heartache and money."
- **The pilot is run by the innovation team and you have limited contact with the business units.** The disconnect between the innovation team and the operations teams that control budgets is always a yellow flag. Escalate and demand insight as to what will come next after the pilot or else qualify out.
- **The customer's team becomes harder to access.** This is an obvious signal that their priorities have changed and/or you are not the priority you used to be. You may be able to work with this but, at some point, you may need to escalate and stop work until you get more engagement.

That time when a startup rejected a $100,000 purchase order.

Once, at one of my companies, the team had negotiated a six-figure pilot with a large, household name. The timeline was tricky but doable, as was the scope. The problem was the lack of success criteria. They weren't crisp on what they were really looking for and what a rollout would look like if we were successful. Another red flag was how difficult it was for us to engage with people outside the innovation team or get any clear answers as to what value they could drive or the path to rollout.

The customer, on a deadline, sent them a PO for the pilot. After some probing, they discovered the source of their urgency: the interns whom the customer had earmarked to handle the project would head back to university in the fall. They decided to walk. Intern timelines as the forcing function signaled that the project wasn't important enough and, in fact, was make-work for the interns. No one wants to reject six-figure POs, but this one had the hallmarks of at least two pilot purgatory modalities, so they made the right call.

WHEN TO CONTINUE OR BOW OUT

Too often, startups fall into pilot purgatory and keep going sideways until it's too late. You have to know when it's time to move on. Be intentional about your pilots and have regular check-ins so that you're always clear on your path forward.

That isn't to say you should quit if things go wrong. Quite the opposite. Keep going if you're making progress against the failure modes, you have confidence in your road map, and there is the right engagement with the customer. But know when to cut your losses if, for instance, you lack belief in success or the opportunity costs are too great. It's tempting to keep going when both parties have sunk costs and reputational risk at stake. In fact, your team won't want to give up (that's why you hired them!). But make the tough call, take the sword out of their hands, and marshal your resources to the opportunities you're better set up to win.

Set yourself up for success before going into your pilots, choose your pilot customers wisely, and don't be afraid to pull the cord if it's not a good fit. Successfully navigating the pilot phase into production is a key milestone on your way to product readiness. Once you've nailed your pilots and proven your business value to the customer, it's time to ensure you get a fair piece of the pie. We'll talk about that next.

CHAPTER 3

COMMIT TO A BUSINESS MODEL

It was June 27, 2019. Walid Halty, the twenty-something founder of Dvinci, a solar marketing automation platform, trudged home after a long day of what was proving to be a long year. Dvinci, Walid's third solar startup, had just favorably settled a bruising lawsuit brought by their biggest customer. But it didn't feel like a victory. Dvinci's coffers were running dry, having spent a small fortune defending the suit. He had to do something.

Dvinci started out providing solar agents and consultants with the tools to sell residential solar. They would then find installers to actually execute the project. It was a slog. Walid had market insight: while photovoltaic panel prices have dropped more than 90 percent in the past decade, the "soft" sales and marketing costs of solar have stayed stubbornly high. That was Dvinci's opportunity. But they were struggling to make it a sustainable business. And then they lost their largest customer.

Undeterred, Walid did what resourceful founders do. He pivoted. Hard.

As Walid recounted, "We asked ourselves, 'What do we have of value? What do we do really well right now that we can monetize?'"

As it turns out, the answer was hiding in plain sight: "We realized we provided a lot of value to installers by bringing them demand. So, we changed our business model to charging for delivering cost-effective leads to solar installers."

Walid pivoted Dvinci to sell leads and software to the same solar installers that had been their suppliers in the old business model. It worked. In the ensuing twelve months, Dvinci went from $0 to a $3 million annual recurring revenue (ARR), leading to a $4 million seed round in November 2020.[16]

Product readiness includes your business model, which describes how you capture value from your product. Fundamentally, your business model answers two questions: how far up the stack do you go and how do you capture fair value at what unit economics?

DETERMINE HOW HIGH UP THE STACK YOU GO

You can adopt a commodity, volume-based model or go way up the stack to provide an end-to-end solution and various permutations in between. There's no right answer to how far up the stack you go. However, you do need a clear answer to move forward. While you may have experimented during the Zero-to-One stage, you will be well served to align on one consistent model to get to Ten. Selling a commodity in one vertical and a solution in another won't be a good look to your Series A VC.

---

16 Impressively, Walid had bootstrapped Dvinci until the seed round. Even more impressive: he had also cold emailed the two VCs, RTP Ventures and CEAS Investments, that ended up leading the seed round.

Let's take my portfolio company, Asylon. Their initial innovation was to sell a battery swap technology to enable higher uptime for drones. They realized that not only was it hard to make a living just selling the component, but it also wasn't what their customers wanted. Their customers didn't want the widget, they wanted a business outcome—in their case, cost-efficient perimeter security. So, Asylon went up the stack to provide aerial security as a service and are capturing more of their fair value. They also decided against going fully up the stack to provide the entire solution, choosing to stay at the subsystem level to provide aerial security and related applications. Instead, they've signed distribution partners like Allied Universal to provide end-to-end physical security incorporating Asylon's DroneCore and DroneIQ products. The following diagram sums up the value to be captured at each level of the stack.[17]

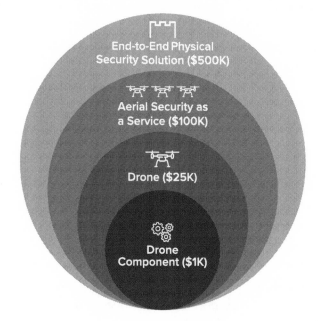

End-to-End Physical
Security Solution ($500K)

Aerial Security as
a Service ($100K)

Drone ($25K)

Drone
Component ($1K)

---

17   The amounts are confidential but I've normalized them to $1 at the component.

It was a great call. Since their shift to the aerial-security-as-a-service business model, they've grown revenues over 1,000 percent and signed up recurring six- and seven-figure contracts with the likes of Ford, FedEx, and Verizon, among others.

Two heuristics to use when deciding where to play in the stack are market maturity and ease of deployment. The less mature a market is, the more likely it is that you'll need to go up the stack. When Asylon came out, there just weren't that many players skilled at drone component integration, so their better battery swap "mousetrap" was best used by themselves to offer their customers a service. On the other hand, take the mature automobile industry where you have suppliers that just provide certain parts that are then integrated into larger subsystems and assemblies. Besides market maturity, pay attention to the ease of deployment of your product. It's easier to stay at one part of the stack when your product is easy to deploy and integrate by the end user. On the other hand, complex integrations and immature technologies beg for more vertical integration. Last, if you do go up the stack, stand up a Professional Services function to help customers and create a buffer for your engineering team. I'll cover that in greater depth in Part 2.

OPERATING A PLATFORM VS. A MANAGED SERVICE

I was recently in a board meeting where one of the strategic questions revolved around whether the company should go into a tech-enabled managed service or stay as a platform. This is a fairly common question facing startups with new technologies. Their customers don't know the tech as well as they do and so will demand more of the startup. Founders then have a choice.

On the one hand, offering a tech-enabled managed service

makes great sense: customers want a job done and you're not doing anyone any favors by just selling picks and shovels when they don't know how to use them. Instead you use what you've built to do the job for the customer. There's a clear path to revenue and it makes for stickier customer relationships. On the other hand, where do you draw the line and at what point do you start looking like a services business to the detriment of your valuation and prospective investors?

Let's say you've built a robotic platform to pick tomatoes. The obvious move is to offer tomato picking as a service to farmers, which is what you've done. You build out infrastructure to manage your fleet of robots, having humans in the loop monitoring the robots. This works so well that the customers then ask you if you could monitor their other fleets of robots using what you've built. How to think about this strategic question?

Will your Managed Service really be tech enabled?

If your people could still deliver a good service without the tech that you've built, that's a good indicator that you're doing a services business. With the example I've given, you couldn't easily do the third-party robotic fleet monitoring without the infrastructure already in place, which is a good indicator. But that's not enough.

Margin counts.

Model out the gross and contribution margins if you do the managed service and what it could be over time. These should be closer to platform margins than services margins and reflect the technology advantage that your platform gives you as well as economies of scale from the infrastructure you've built out.

Take Palantir, long denigrated as a services business in software clothing. According to their S1, their gross margins were close to 80 percent in 2020 when excluding stock-based compensation.[18] They go on to note:

> The improvements in our operating results have principally been driven by a significant decrease in the time and number of software engineers required to install, deploy, and manage our software platforms...We have also invested heavily in developing the infrastructure used to deliver software updates to our customers, which has increased the number of upgrades our engineers can manage across installations...

Palantir has built a massive business providing tech-enabled managed services.

Ease of deployment and quick time to value lend themselves to staying as a platform.

Think Amazon S3 or Airtable. They no doubt had customers that wanted them to do more but it made sense to stay horizontal and educate their customers instead because there's such quick time to value.

"Oligopsonies" lend themselves to managed services.

If there are a limited number of buyers in a market, tech-enabled managed services will help you stay sticky with your customers while shutting the competition out. The big warehouse management systems like Manhattan Associates used this playbook back in the day to be essential to their customers.

---

18   "Palantir Technologies Inc. Form S-1 Registration Statement," Securities and Exchange Commission, August 25, 2020, 88, https://www.sec.gov/Archives/edgar/data/1321655/000119312520230013/d904406ds1.htm.

Don't fight the market.

There are some markets and customers for which you just have to provide the service or you won't be in the game. Selling a platform for them to use will fall on deaf ears. In these cases, see the market for what it is and embrace it. This was often the case in adtech. Ad agencies wanted to allocate media, not learn all these various adtech platforms to optimize their spend. So these adtech startups had teams of employees working the knobs and levers of their platform on behalf of their customers. As the market matures, your customers may come 'round to wanting to use the tools themselves. But don't force the issue.

Back to the robotic tomato-picking company. Using the principles below, it'd be a no-brainer to expand their platform and operations to include third-party robotic fleet monitoring.

In summary, you can build a big business doing tech-enabled managed services. Just make sure they're truly tech-enabled, which will be reflected in your margins.

OPTIMIZE YOUR PRICING MODEL AND POLICIES

Pricing is a signal and reflects your value proposition. You may have tried a number of pricing models during the Zero-to-One phase. You'll want to narrow these for your next phase. There's lots of literature dedicated solely to pricing, and I address unit economics in the next chapter, so I won't go deep, but consider the following pricing principles.

Consolidate pricing models.

As you build out a go-to-market team, it will be confusing to have more than two pricing models. Think of a model as a way of charging. You may charge per user, per transaction, or per some other action. While you may have tiers within a pricing model (for example, silver, gold, and platinum levels), the way you charge should not change.

Use pricing to differentiate your value proposition.

Are there ways you can differentiate your product via pricing differently? Common methods involve sharing risk and upside with the customer, keying off another variable, or dramatically undercutting the competition.

For example, in the stodgy, cyclical world of manufacturing, Plex, the private equity-backed enterprise resource planning software company, has used pricing to differentiate themselves. Their pricing is based on the customer's revenues, and thus ties their success to that of the customer. So, you'll pay more as your revenue grows and pay less if you have a bad year.

Pricing should align with product value and sales motion.

While it may sound obvious, avoid imbalances in pricing compared to product value and sales motion. For instance, selling $30,000 licenses in yearlong sales cycles by an expensive field sales force will kill your business. One startup I work with has a product that they can comfortably sell at a $150,000 annual contract value (ACV). Some investors have been asking how they can get to $1 million ACV. The fact is, the current iteration of their product's value proposition can't support that price point. Having acknowledged this, they are planning their go-to-market to go after more volume while making product investments to increase ACV in future years.

Increase prices until customers say they're too high.

Startups tend to underprice their products. They want those big logos to help with fundraising and recruiting, which is understandable. However, to customers, a lower price may also signal a lack of confidence in the value proposition. When a prospect says it's too high, ask them to explain why. They'll "play your value back" to you, which can be invaluable in understanding how they perceive your value proposition.

I remember one analytics startup that started with a $1,000 per month price point for their first customers. They then consistently raised the price until the customers refused to pay. By the end, they landed between $4,000 and $6,000 per month subscriptions. The pricing held until they got acquired, letting them know they had found the right pricing for the value they offered customers.

Pricing too low can be worse than being too high.

Remember, pricing is a signal. Price too low and you risk sending the message that you don't have confidence in your offering. Yes, buyers want a good ROI and to feel like they're getting a good deal. But they'll be suspicious if something is priced too low. The savviest buyers also want to make sure their suppliers are viable. They don't want suppliers to overextend themselves as it will only come back to haunt them.

I'll never forget the first large business purchase I was ever involved with. It was a project to store data and have it available for business intelligence back when these were big, on-premise software purchases. One of the key components was an extract, transform, load (ETL) platform. We had the leading companies at the time in to pitch us. Our database engineers had a clear favorite, Informatica. Their rep had driven up in her convertible Porsche with her sales engineer and impressed us with their pitch and demo. She quoted us $100,000 for the license plus support.

We narrowed it down to Informatica and one other company. The engineers had a clear preference for Informatica and so we flagged this to the other contender. They immediately offered to waive the entire cost of their license. We could have their software if we just paid for the ongoing support and maintenance, which would be $20,000 a year, and agreed to a case study. We went back to the Informatica rep to negotiate the deal down, but she wouldn't budge.

What were we to do? We sucked it up and went with Informatica. The contender, whose name I don't even remember, flagged a lack of belief in their product by dropping their price so quickly and drastically. Meanwhile, the Informatica rep oozed confidence in her proposition and its fit to our problem. She got the business and deservedly so. No wonder she drove a Porsche.

Make discounts explicit.

You may need to drop your price or give additional value to win a deal. In these cases, make sure the customer knows the value they're getting (i.e., note the discount in the proposal) so as not to anchor them to the lower pricing. And don't discount too heavily without justification or risk your credibility as described above.

Use price to overcome adoption friction and match it to the value you add.

Often, the installation of your solution will be high friction. It will require many hours to install and calibrate. It might require even more time for the customer to integrate into their own systems. This friction, though inevitable, prevents customers from realizing the value of your solution, especially early on. You can overcome the friction with pricing options like pricing services at low or no margin, enabling the customer to pay the install fees over time or with their ongoing payments, or volume discounts for your bigger, enterprise customers.

Use price/commitment to qualify customer demand.

Test the buyer's motivation using pricing as a tool. For instance, at one of my companies, they'd have original equipment manufacturer (OEM) prospects asking for certain types of guarantees such as the right to manufacture (RTM) the products should there be supply issues. These are reasonable asks, but not something to give away freely. As a compromise, they adopted a minimum spend construct spelling out that they wouldn't entertain RTM unless it was a seven-figure minimum annual spend. They deliberately added this barrier to discern those who were serious about designing them in from those that weren't as far along.

Consider "flipping" the model.

Are there opportunities to give away part of your product to differentiate and drive adoption while capturing value elsewhere? Dvinci flipped their model by focusing on lead generation. Toast, the multibillion-dollar restaurant tech company, makes as much revenue from facilitating payments as they do from their flagship point-of-sale product. If bringing revenue in feels like too much of a slog for too little payback, like it did for

Dvinci, you'll want to think of flipping your model. Take Packy McCormick, writer of the popular *Not Boring* newsletter, which focuses on business strategy and pop culture. It's notoriously hard to make money writing. What was Packy to do? Besides selling sponsorships to his newsletters, he offers his audience opportunities to invest in the companies he covers and will capture meaningful upside from doing so.[19]

Use value-based pricing to capture more value.

My wife and I experienced a curious phenomenon after we bought our house. Contractor prices would magically be higher for the job when they learned our zip code (we moved to an affluent town). Same job, same team, different price for us than in a surrounding town. This is value-based pricing. You price based on the value of your product to the customer. Value-based pricing works best for larger-ticket items that are sold top-down, i.e., it's tough to do in a bottom-up, product-led growth model.

At Videoplaza, we sold into the highly commoditized ad-serving market where there was a race to the bottom in terms of the cost to serve a thousand impressions (CPM). The incumbent ad-serving platforms priced between one cent and ten cents depending on volume, whereas we charged twenty cents to fifty cents plus. You read that right.

We priced based on value. Our prices were higher for broadcasters in richer countries that could afford and justify the higher CPM for best-in-class video ad serving. And we priced lower in countries like India and Spain that didn't have high advertising rates to begin with, or for ad networks that had lower margins.

---

19   Packy McCormick, "A Not Boring Adventure, One Year In," Not Boring, April 5, 2021, https://www. notboring.co/p/a-not-boring-adventure-one-year-in.

We were thus able to price discriminate based on type of customer and geography.

How you price should reflect where you are in the stack, the value customers derive from your product, and the competition. For instance, as long as Asylon focuses on aerial security, their product will be compared to other means of security, whether humans or stationary cameras. You'll know you're capturing your fair share when winning deals feels like less of a slog. Next in the quest for product readiness is to get your scalability ducks in a row.

CHAPTER 4

INVEST IN SCALABILITY

When he said, "If you are not embarrassed by the first version of your product, you've launched too late," Reid Hoffman was referring to the Zero-to-One phase, which is all about doing things that don't scale. From personally onboarding each customer to handcrafting units, these unscalable activities are important to understand your value proposition as you discover product–market fit. This calculus changes as you go from One to Ten. You can't scrap your way to scalability. This means a shift in mindset to investing in scalability, which is at the heart of product readiness.

While scalability starts with technology, it encompasses a number of functions beyond the core product itself. There are a number of "jobs to be done" that may or may not need a full-time person to do them.[20] Regardless, you'll want to explicitly designate ownership of these or else they'll fall through the cracks and impact product readiness. I've put together a list of the functions most likely to be overlooked. You'll need to find

---

20 A framework made famous by Clay Christensen, https://hbr.org/2016/09/
know-your-customers-jobs-to-be-done.

owners for these to get to Ten, but it's by no means a comprehensive list.

CUSTOMER EXPERIENCE/A DAY IN THE LIFE

Engineering teams tend to hyperfocus on the components or subsystems of a product. While that improves the technical quality of your solution, it can sometimes be a detriment to the overall customer experience. Don't let this be an afterthought. How will the customer experience your product? Will they receive it in a box, via your field application engineering (FAE) team, or through crisp, clear documentation? What will Day One look like? Day Thirty? And what will their touchpoints be? Product management or product marketing usually owns this. If not, you should own it.

Think through the customer experience and be deliberate about what you want to achieve. Small gestures count. At Videoplaza, we would celebrate a customer go-live by sending co-branded cupcakes to the teams that were responsible for the implementation. It reinforced our competitive positioning as the company that would stay close to our customers and provide the best service.

CUSTOMER INTEGRATION POINTS

Customers integrate products into other platforms or processes via an application programming interface (API) or a software development kit (SDK), or physically via I/O such as Ethernet or USB. These integration points are often an afterthought in a startup's product development process that can come back to haunt you. Integration points should be first-class citizens when it comes to the time spent designing and testing them.

Poor integration points detract from your value proposition and can disproportionately affect customer happiness.

OPERATIONS AND CUSTOMER SUPPORT

Make it clear who will handle customer support tickets and field operations. If your engineers have been handling these to date, you will need to break this out into a separate team as you land more customers. Put a ticketing system like Jira in place if you don't already have one.

DOCUMENTATION

By that same token, poor documentation can take the bloom off your product. Again, this is often an afterthought when engineering is grinding to hit a deadline. Incomplete documentation leads to more unneeded support requests. At Videoplaza, I insisted that a product wasn't shippable unless both internal- and external-facing documentation were in place and tested. Insist on the same.

QUALITY ASSURANCE

Testing and Quality Assurance are obviously integral to hardening your product for scale. It's tempting to reduce testing time to make a deadline or to rely on the engineering team to do their own testing. There are serious trade-offs to weigh when you decide how much testing is enough, which I'll cover in the next chapter.

If you make hardware, you will eventually need a Quality Assurance function. Make them responsible for product reliability and have them involved across the product lifecycle from design to testing to manufacturing and finally in life. Early on, manufacturing and quality can be combined, but you'll want to separate these over time so there are the right checks and balances.

MANUFACTURING AND SUPPLY CHAIN

Product readiness in hardware startups hinges on engineering design, testing, and manufacturing. Don't skimp on the latter. Your head of manufacturing will be responsible for procuring the materials to build your products, managing and negotiating pricing with suppliers, and, well, getting stuff built and out the door. They should also be involved upstream with Engineering during the design process, whether to advise on components or on manufacturing processes. You will want to understand if Engineering is planning to use components that are hard to come by or will soon be obsolete. The Manufacturing function can also inform the design process in what's called DFM.[21] Moreover, this function should work downstream with Finance to optimize the bill of materials (BOM) that will drive your cost of goods sold (COGS) and thus your gross margins.

PROFESSIONAL SERVICES

Professional Services is one of the most misunderstood, and undervalued, functions in an enterprise technology startup.[22] Here's how the story usually plays out:

---

21 Design for manufacturing.

22 In fact, PS revenues are often a big percentage of revenues and scale with your revenues. Benchmark Capital General Partner Chetan Puttagunta tweeted about PS making up ~ 46 percent of revenues for Veeva and Workday at $60 million in revenues, going down to ~ 20 percent of revenues at $800 million. He went on to tweet: "[PS] is absolutely underrated. Professional services in order to deeply engage large enterprise customers are often necessary."

Founders think, "Providing services is messy, low-margin work. Why do that when we have APIs and SDKs that our customers or their dev shops can use to integrate our product? And having lots of services revenues will kill our valuation." Fast-forward a few months. They sign their first customers. Inevitably, they underestimate the integration involved. Their APIs weren't mature, the documentation wasn't up to snuff. Whatever the case, the company needs to pull out the stops to make these first customers referenceable. So, the engineering team gets pulled in, having to get on calls, do remote support, or, God forbid, go on site. This wasn't baked into the road map so velocity stalls out, the customers are unhappy, the sales team distracted. Several board meetings later, the founder relents and stands up a PS team.

You want your engineers to be doing the first installs. This helps them understand the customer experience and develops customer empathy. It's also a forcing function to build robust customer integration points. But after your first few customers, you need to protect the core engineering team from customer integration work. That's where PS comes in.

Our PS team at Videoplaza, led by the formidable Oscar Wall, was our secret weapon. They saved a number of large accounts that threatened to churn to the competition, all while helping us go on offense to win new accounts and generating incremental revenues. Here's what worked well for us:

- Our PS team also performed presales engineering. There was the benefit of continuity with the same team that scoped out a solution being responsible for its delivery, and we pooled our resources for more flexibility.
- PS projects should use existing product integration points.

PS should NOT be building new integration points. That can lead to PS developing a competing product. I've seen that movie and it didn't end well.

- PS should be priced profitably but not overly so. At Videoplaza, we deliberately ran PS at breakeven. We assumed we'd need to give away PS hours to win deals or keep existing accounts happy—easy to justify given our margins and customer lifetime values. This impacted that group's margin, but they understood their strategic role. Had we tried to maximize profitability, they'd have run themselves more like an agency, leading to misalignment.
- View PS engagements as permission to learn more from the customer. We had two instances where custom work for one customer went on to become productized in the core platform, becoming seven-figure businesses within a year.
- Consider rotating PS staff with Engineering. It's helpful for engineers to be "at the coalface" for a while, and, vice versa, having PS engineers in the shoes of their platform colleagues can build empathy and relationships that will stand you in good stead.

So, embrace PS. You'll find that customers that engage PS are happier and larger than those that don't.

PRODUCT MARKETING

Another perennially underrated capability, Product Marketing positions your product in the market and quarterbacks its launch. You likely already have some references and messaging that you've used on your first customers. The primary focus of your Product Marketing team should be on:

- **Product Positioning:** From product naming to messaging to framing the competitive landscape, it's important to shape a crisp, high-level story of your product, the differentiated value proposition, and the buyer personas.

- **Sales Enablement:** You'll be building out a sales team. They will first need to be "sold" on your product before they can sell to customers. You'll need sales tools such as demo videos, presentations, case studies, ROI calculators, rate cards, objection handling FAQs, and the like to train the sales team.
- **Product Launch:** Devise a product launch plan and execute on it. Will it be a "lightning strike" event at a trade show? A rolling soft launch? A roadshow? While every context differs, the following principles can help you think this through:
  - Bias toward public launches, whether physical or virtual. You're more likely to break through the noise by focusing your energies on a moment instead of diffusion. Public launches galvanize teams to work toward a committed deadline. It feels great to work tirelessly and pull off a big launch.
  - Don't launch without at least a few solid case studies and referenceable customers. No one reads product press releases with no customers in them.
  - Consider recruiting analysts to support a launch via a white paper or webinar. This is an underutilized tactic that can be particularly effective to establish credibility.
  - Roadshows work well when you're selling top-down to a smaller customer set. Roadshows were effective at Brightcove and Videoplaza, whereas trade shows are a better vehicle for, say, robotics startups selling to automation engineers.

Don't skimp on product marketing. As Tomasz Tunguz, VC at Redpoint Ventures, put it:

Over the past decade or so, I've found hiring a product marketer first leads to more consistent success. Why is this?

Though the startup may have achieved product–market fit, the company may not understand the fit. Who is using the product and why? How does the buyer journey evolve with time? How do buyers describe the product amongst each other? Few early-stage companies can answer those questions accurately.

Establishing this foundation enables the company to determine which messages to proclaim and which customers to pursue. Having this framework aligns the business and typically increases marketing efficiency because campaigns are well-targeted and resonate better. Demand generation and brand marketers will reap the benefits of this work. So will the rest of the business because it deeply understands its customers.[23]

TECH DEBT AND UNIT ECONOMICS

"We built a four-bedroom house. We were able to fit ten people inside. It was starting to get crowded. Fast-forward a few quarters and we had to fit a hundred people on that same plot. It doesn't mean that the first house was poorly constructed, but at that point we needed an apartment complex."

That's Tareef Kawaf, President of RStudio and Brightcove's first VP of Engineering. He's describing that moment during our journey from One to Ten where our growth combined with our technical debt forced us to refactor the platform. It set us back at least a year in terms of new feature development, but it had to be done.

---

23 Tomasz Tunguz, "The Most Frequent Mishire in Startups," November 10, 2019, https://tomtunguz.com/most-frequent-mishire.

You've undoubtedly incurred your share of tech debt during the Zero-to-One phase. Plan to pay it down during the One-to-Ten phase. That doesn't mean stopping new development to focus on retiring all debt. It does mean baking it into your road map even if it means making hard trade-offs.

Startups chasing growth and new logos tend to overinvest in new features and underinvest in retiring technical debt. This debt inevitably catches up, causing them to blow up their road map or worse. Just ask Tareef. He was made to prioritize new features and products every single time and it came back to bite us. Luckily, we had enough momentum and resources to overcome this.

Last, besides system capacity and uptime, technical debt also manifests itself in unit economics. You may not have optimized for unit economics to date, but you'll need to invest in this during the One-to-Ten phase, for instance in projects to improve gross margins. Unit economics really start to count with Series A and, especially, Series B investors.

You've got your scalability ducks in a row. If you're already in production, skip the next chapter and go to Part 2. If you're still in beta or pilots, read on. You need to decide when to shoot the engineer.

CHAPTER 5

SHIP YOUR PRODUCT

"Instead of letting it sit in a lab for five years and creating this robotic application before it's finally ready to deploy to the real world, we deployed it today. It's not fully autonomous—it's autonomous maybe 90, 95% of the time. The other 5–10% is assisted by remote human operators, but it's reliable on day one, and it's reliable on day 10,000."[24]

—SIMON KALOUCHE, FOUNDER AND CEO, NIMBLE ROBOTICS

Deciding when your product is "good enough" to ship is one of the most important calls you'll make during the One-to-Ten stage.

Ship something half-baked and you'll have your engineering team fighting fires, your customers unhappy, your go-to-market staff demoralized. Wait too long and you risk overengineering the product, lengthening the time to get customer feedback, ultimately shortening your runway. Do not delegate this decision to your team. You will own it either way.

---

24   Brian Heater, "Nimble Robotics scores $50M for its fulfillment automation tech," TechCrunch, March 11, 2021, https://techcrunch.com/2021/03/11/nimble-robotics-scores-50m-for-its-fulfillment-automation-tech.

DECIDE WHEN YOUR PRODUCT IS GOOD ENOUGH

How do you know when it's the right time? In hardware, you may be using a product lifecycle (PLC) framework, also known as the V-model. It builds in accountability, via periodic design and program reviews, and defined entry/exit criteria for each stage.

Besides a formal PLC framework, use the following heuristics to decide when to ship:

- **Churn reduction/table stakes.** Address the reasons for churn of any beta customers or else you'll constantly "fill the bucket" with customers only to have them leak away over time. Early customers churn due to a lack of table stakes features or because they're not getting enough value for the existing product relative to their other options (see Bossa Nova/Walmart). Consistently losing deals involving your ICP is a good indicator that the product isn't quite ready.
- **Uptime or performance KPIs.** This is self-evident. If you're hitting the metrics you need to hit to add value to customers, you are there. The KPIs can involve cost savings, revenue increase, or just usage of your platform. As for uptime, every industry is different. Whereas robotics deployments may get away with 95 percent uptime, mission-critical systems of record need to hit at least four nines (99.99 percent or higher).
- **Repeatability.** How easy is it to stand your product up in multiple locations, customers, instances? You may still be building your own hardware and selling these as revenue units, but do you have a path to being able to use a contract manufacturer? Is your supply chain robust enough to handle the additional volume? Are your integration points robust enough? There isn't one metric to assess repeatability. Rather,

conduct thought exercises to stress test your product: If your largest customer grew 2x tomorrow, what would happen? What if you signed all of your pipeline in the next month? If that kind of growth would break your system or involve a lot of manual work, it's a good indicator of tech debt to retire.

- **Tech debt and scalability.** Acknowledge the debt you have and how it might impact churn or scalability. For instance, maybe your team members were like "squirrels in a box" scurrying to solve problems in the background for your beta customers when these tasks should be automated. You can brute force this for a while, but eventually you'll need to spend engineering cycles on scalability.
- **Customer happiness.** Your pilot customers are important barometers for product readiness. Don't just ask them; see how they're actually using your product.
- **Team sentiment.** By that same token, take the temperature of your team. I put a lot of stock in team confidence. Hopefully you've created a culture where they're comfortable offering candid feedback. The worst outcome is if they tell you what they think you want to hear when they don't believe in the product's readiness.

CONWAY'S LAW: PAY ATTENTION TO THE INTEGRATION POINTS

In 1967, computer programmer Mel Conway introduced the adage, "Any organization that designs a system (defined broadly) will produce a design whose structure is a copy of the organization's communication structure." In other words, you ship your organization chart.[25]

---

25   A more memorable phrase credited to Steven Sinofsky, formerly of Microsoft, now with Andreessen Horowitz.

There is no ideal way to organize teams. You will incur trade-offs any which way you go about it. Regardless of how you've organized your company, pay the most attention to the integration points, where the work product of different teams comes together. That's where the most system failures happen because each team may be locally optimizing while achieving a suboptimal result at a system level. That's also where Systems Engineering plays its valuable role in taking a holistic view across the components and making the tough trade-offs.

SHOOT THE ENGINEER

Engineers tend to want to, well, engineer stuff. They'll especially want to do so if they'll be on the hook for customer support. Sometimes they just like tinkering when there's no real difference to customers. I once met an engineer who, late one night, was showing me his work, his tinkering. I asked him when it'd be ready to ship. He hemmed and hawed and then talked about shooting the engineer. Huh?

He told me about an old saying: "There comes a time on every project when you just have to shoot the engineer and get it out the door."[26] This is natural. Engineers tend to want to optimize and develop what's next on the road map. You'll want to give them space to do their work and air any misgivings they may have so their voice has been heard, balanced with the clamor from customers and sales to get the product out there. Use the heuristics above to come to a decision that the product is ready to ship, ideally bringing your team along the way. If there are still doubts, ultimately it's your job as CEO to understand the risks you'll face in shipping the version you have and draw the

---

26 Ironically, this from an engineer known for his brilliance and also his incessant tinkering!

line as to what's good enough to ship. And once you've made the call, once you've shot the engineers, you'll need to own the results. You'll lose your team's respect if you don't.

You've proven customer value, you're able to capture a fair share of it, and you're confident in your ability to scale the product. Congratulations on achieving product readiness, the first leg of the stool to get from One to Ten. Next up: building a repeatable sales machine.

PART 2

BUILD A
REPEATABLE
SALES MACHINE

Meet James Richards, founder of Teleborder. He and Teleborder were flying high in 2014. A graduate of the legendary Y Combinator, James got to $1 million in revenue and convinced Khosla Ventures to lead their $3 million seed round.

Two years later, he "landed the Teleborder plane" at TriNet in an acquihire.

What happened?

"We weren't able to get beyond me selling our deals. We built out a sales team with demand generation but the results didn't follow. At the same time, we'd ramped up burn and had shortened our runway. It was then about landing the plane somewhere safe."

Founder-led sales are key during the Zero-to-One stage: you are the visionary. You can best articulate the problem you're solving to convince the early adopters. Moreover, it's important for you to have the direct link to the customer to hone your value proposition.

But that won't get you to Ten and beyond. You'll need to build a repeatable sales machine. VCs call this go-to-market fit and it's key to unlocking your next round of funding. Show that your team can predictably and repeatedly sell your product, and you'll be on your way to your Series A or B.

From honing your sales motion to reliably generating demand to improving sales execution, building a repeatable sales machine entails putting processes into place to optimize for predictability. I'll cover these in the following chapters. The last chapter in Part 2 covers hiring, perhaps the most important aspect of a repeatable sales machine. While much of Part 2 is applicable to all businesses, it's geared toward those with top-down enterprise sales motions, which can particularly be challenging for technical founders.

Remember, repeatable sales require product marketing that we covered in Part 1. You'll need customer-facing materials (sales decks, demos, pricing, contracts) as well as internal-facing materials (sales scripts, rate cards, objection handling, and the like). Most importantly, repeatable sales imply referenceable customers. If you don't have referenceable customers, you're likely still in the Zero-to-One stage. Put this book down. Go make your customers referenceable and then come back.

CHAPTER 6

HONE YOUR SALES MOTION

"We essentially put an end to pilots and doubled down on e-commerce customers."

That's Amy Villeneuve again, talking about how they streamlined Kiva's motion to unlock greater sales velocity. Previously, the team was trying to be all things to all people, chasing deals across sectors and diluting their efforts. Worse, since the ticket price for a Kiva system could run to tens of millions of dollars, customers understandably demanded pilots, resulting in much lengthier sales cycles.

Amy streamlined the Kiva sales motion to only focus on e-commerce customers, where the growth really was, and raised the bar to work with Kiva. Instead, they'd invite prospects to visit existing customers to see their technology at work. "We actually didn't call them pilots anymore. The smallest sales we would do was $1.5 million." This radically shortened the sales cycle and also served as a way to qualify new prospects.

DETERMINE YOUR SALES MOTION

Your sales motion defines how you sell and to whom, taking into account your product, its pricing, and the type and frequency of touchpoints required to close a sale. You may have experimented with multiple motions during the Zero-to-One phase. You'll want to commit to one during the One-to-Ten phase. It's tough to do more than one motion in parallel when you're sub-scale. I'll start with a basic framework for understanding sales motions, followed by some principles on streamlining them.

There are fundamentally three types of sale motions with all kinds of variations in between:

- **Product-led/freemium.** These tend to be self-serve products that the buyer can adopt without talking to a human. Think Dropbox, Airtable, and Slack.[27] Self-serve tends to work for low-friction products costing hundreds to low thousands of dollars per year.
- **Inside sales/high-velocity sales.** This motion involves remote human contact to consult with the buyer and facilitate the transaction. Free trials and demos are often used to help the customer in their evaluation; however, it's still a relatively light touch. High-velocity sales motions tend to involve deals in the five figures with sales cycles taking on the order of weeks. HubSpot, Toast, and Zendesk are good examples here.
- **Field/top-down sales.** This is the more "traditional" sales motion of having field sales teams on-site at customers' locations.[28] These sales cycles tend to be longer and more

---

27 Even the most frictionless, self-serve, bottom-up companies like these need enterprise sales teams to achieve growth.

28 The aftereffects of the COVID-19 pandemic make on-site visits less frequent, but physical interaction for large deals won't go away.

complex, involving relationship building and multiple touch-points with deals that can take quarters if not years to close. Enterprise deals, which are most of what you'll find here, should be worth at least six figures for any given customer.

Product-led and high-velocity sales motions are highly quantitative, indeed formulaic, and easier for nonsales founders to grok. On the other hand, the top-down sales motion involves a lot more uncertainty with longer, more complex processes and bigger deal sizes, and so I'll focus more on this one. The top-down sales motion can be further broken out in terms of channel, sector, and process.

SALES CHANNEL

Most often, your reps will sell directly to the end users of the technology. As we've discussed, equipping your reps with the best value propositions for each customer segment is critical as you start to scale. Many enterprise startups start off selling direct due to having a direct link to the end user, a faster sales cycle, and being able to control their own destiny and not being dependent on a third party.

That said, some products lend themselves to indirect distribution such as via original equipment manufacturer (OEM) sales. OEM customers embed your product into their product. These sales require "design wins" where the OEM selects your product to go into their offering. Chip and sensor businesses tend to be OEM-based sales. OEM cycles are longer than direct because you are convincing someone else to bake your product into theirs, which they will in turn sell to others. However, once the partnership is established, revenues can scale quickly as so much of the work has been done upfront.

Similarly, systems integrators drive sales by integrating your product, perhaps with some customization, and "stitching together" the solution for the end user. Be selective when choosing solutions partners as each one will require investment in signing, onboarding, and integration.

SECTOR

Each sector has its unique characteristics that you'll need to think through when architecting your motion. For instance, media and advertising have an element of "co-opetition." Publishers that are rivals in attracting audiences may work together in, say, joining a network to combine their inventory to sell to advertisers. As such, publishers will like to hear that you're working with their peers. Sales and marketing tactics here may involve webinars, joint dinners, and the like, and it's heavy on relationships.

On the other hand, I was recently involved with a startup selling to commodities trading desks. In that world, any information edge can translate into millions of dollars, so they hate the idea that you may be working with their peers. Needless to say, webinars and group dinners would not be effective tactics in this sector.

PROCESS

Your sales process breaks down the stages from qualifying a new lead to closing it. Let's take the examples below:

Enterprise SaaS: This represents a plain vanilla enterprise software sell. The Solution Design phase involves scoping out an integration and can happen in parallel with the commercial negotiation.

Discovery → Qualification → Demo → Technical
Win → Solution Design → Negotiation → Close

Robotics System to End User: Now let's say you're selling a robotics system to warehouse operators. You may have one negotiation for the pilot contract and then another one for the production rollout. And there may be more hoops to jump through, such as the Infosec audit if you pass the pilot phase. Again, some of these can happen in parallel but are shown in serial for simplicity's sake.

Discovery → Qualification → Demo → PoC →
Solution Design → Negotiation → Pilot → Infosec
Audit / Credit Check / Negotiation → Close

Sensor System to OEM: This example involves selling your sensor system to OEMs to embed in their products. OEM sales, and Systems Integrator sales for that matter, involve the two-step of first getting the design win and then sales of the combined product or solution.

Discovery → Qualification → Evaluation Kit
→ Solution Design → Design Win → Pilot →
Supply Agreement Negotiation → Close

RATIONALIZE YOUR SALES FUNNEL

Use a funnel to visually represent your process and calibrate. Following are two funnels representing two of my previous companies.

The one on the left is akin to what we had at Videoplaza, where we were selling a mission-critical monetization capability to digital video publishers and would "rip and replace" their existing ad-serving platform. Our volume-based pricing model meant that the lion's share of our revenue was driven by the very large broadcasters. So the top of our funnel was relatively narrow. There were only so many publishers in a territory that would move the needle. We had to build relationships with each of them, evangelizing, sometimes for years, until they would commit to an evaluation, either as a pilot or a formal request for proposal (RFP). That's when we knew the account was in play. Evaluations were costly to support, so we had to have a good win rate coming out of these.[29]

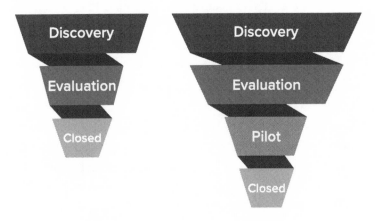

The one on the right looks more like what an internet-of-things (IoT) startup with a more horizontal product would have. The funnel is wider since their product can be integrated into various applications by end users, systems integrators, or OEMs, and serviced via evaluation kits sold by an inside sales team. There will then be some customers/partners that wish to proceed with pilots at the systems level, and the funnel gets a lot narrower for these. Even more than software businesses, the

---

29   Ours ranged from 50 to 80 percent, depending on the market and the year.

conversion from pilot to win for hardware-based businesses should be 80 percent or more. It's just too expensive to do pilots that don't result in a win.

Streamline your motion via the following heuristics.

Repeatable sales require the honing of your sales motion. Up until now, perhaps you've been feeling your way on deals. That won't get you to Ten. While your VP of sales may be writing the detailed playbook, use the following heuristics to assess and streamline your sales motion.

Focus on one motion at the get-go.

Companies at scale such as Toast, Workday, and Salesforce. com have multiple sales. They have offerings targeting horizontal and vertical segments and teams that cater to each one. Obviously, they have the scale to do this; right now, you don't. Stick to one sales motion in the beginning so as to not dilute your sales and marketing resources across multiple motions. One exception is where you sell evaluation versions of your product via e-commerce or inside sales. You then engage more deeply with those customers that have successfully evaluated your product.

Don't confuse demo/proof of concept with pilot.

Early into an advisee engagement with Butlr, a thermal-sensor-based person-monitoring system, their founder, Honghao Deng, scheduled a call with me to discuss their pilots. They were stressed, being pulled in many directions by customers and their pilot projects. It took too long to stand up a pilot and they were getting bogged down.

It turns out they had top-of-the-funnel leads for whom they were going straight to pilot before properly qualifying the fit. They were mixing the demo/PoC stage, where you're simply proving that the technology works, with the pilot, where you're proving the value in the customer's environment. This was easily addressed with an evaluation kit to sell to the top of the funnel while diving deeper on accounts that have qualified into the pilot stage.

Refuse pilots after you have enough references for an application.

Remember what Amy Villeneuve did at Kiva Systems. Pilots are to prove value. You don't need them when you've already proven value with reference customers and their case studies or, even better, those reference customers are willing to host your potential customers at their facility to show off your application. You'll still need pilots for new applications of your technology, but push back and have them buy your system if the value has been proven out. Or else raise the dollar threshold for a pilot if the customer insists on testing it in their environment.

Align targets and methods: Elephants, deer, and rabbits. Shotgun or rifle?

The bigger the target, the riskier the hunt.[30] The more horizontal and low-friction your platform, the more of a shotgun approach you'll take in terms of lead generation. Conversely, if yours is a complex technology, you will want to take a much more targeted approach so as not to waste sales cycles.

Christoph Janz, of Point Nine Capital, lays out the number of

---

30   Apologies for the hunting metaphor; fishing metaphors work too.

accounts to get to $100 million ARR based on average revenue per account.[31] You will need to commit to an animal as you find your way from One to Ten, with the exception at the top end where elephants and whales tend to be easier to hunt with the same motion.

Five Ways to Build a $100M SaaS Business

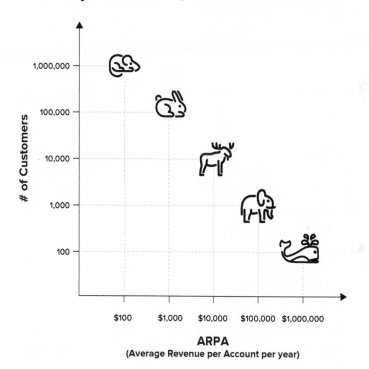

At Videoplaza, in any given country, we targeted the top handful of broadcasters and publishers. We'd realized that it wasn't profitable to work with smaller publishers. The effort to sell and migrate them didn't justify the revenues and opportunity costs.

---

31   Christoph Janz, "Five years later: Five ways to build a $100 million SaaS business," *The Angel VC* (blog), April 7, 2019, http://christophjanz.blogspot.com/2019/04/five-years-later-five-ways-to-build-100.html.

There may be an issue with your business model if you need multiple meetings and demos, and a monthslong process, to close a $40,000 sale. The only way this can work is if you're executing a logo land grab to then land and expand. Speaking of which...

Logo land grab. Land and expand.

This strategy involves deliberately grabbing market share, even if unprofitable at first, and betting on increasing customer lifetime value via organic account growth and new products. This approach especially makes sense when there is a market window to take advantage of.

This was the case at Videoplaza: as YouTube gained steam and advertising budgets flowed online, every publisher and broadcaster needed to up their digital video game. At the same time, in our home markets of Europe and Asia, there was little presence from our American competitors, who were then focused on the massive US market. We knew that it'd only be a matter of time until they would go overseas and be a force to reckon with. So, we went for a land grab strategy, trying to sign as many logos as possible, knowing that we might not be profitable with some of them for a while, if ever. It worked. We were able to lock up many markets in Europe and Asia, which became part of the business case for our acquisition.

Bias toward selling direct, especially in new markets.

Selling direct means you control your own destiny and aren't dependent on channel partners one step removed from your product. What's more, new technologies require evangelization to end customers, which you can do much better than channel partners. You'll also want the direct connection to the end user to capture feedback and deeply understand your value proposition.

If you wish to sell direct but have channel partners "in the way," opt to co-sell or do lead sharing with them.

There may be instances in which selling direct is impractical or unfeasible: the end user may have a systems integrator that is essentially part of their extended team, or there is a group of solution providers that serve as prime contractors for their customers. In these cases, maintain a connection with the end user and co-sell or have the transaction go through the partner.

This was the case during my time in the online video space in which the heavily regulated broadcaster relied on their prime contractors to take on large pieces of work for liability reasons. They'd issue RFPs but instruct the primes to partner with the technology companies they were most interested in using. We pitched together and collaborated on pricing but made sure we maintained the customer connection.

If you decide to sell via indirect channels, go all in.

Selling via indirect channels can give you real leverage, whether in terms of geographical or sector coverage, or else by providing services that you would be hard-pressed to provide. Still, don't underestimate the cost of recruiting, onboarding, and managing channel partners. Channel-based motions also involve product road map investments that you'll need to prioritize over other features—for example, access control and permissions across accounts, billing, and provisioning and customer support tools.

Last, your partner's sales team should be viewed as an extension of your own. Programmatically invest in training, supporting, and incentivizing them to sell your product. Do not take this lightly. It's hard enough to train your own salespeople on what you do, let alone a distributed sales force at a partner selling a number of other products in their portfolio.

Be prescriptive with customers.

Customers often need to be taught on how to buy your product. This is especially true when there are new technologies or processes involved. They won't ask the right questions or have the right stakeholders involved to understand the value or ensure success. Be prescriptive and walk your customer through how to properly evaluate and buy your product. This can be in the form of checklists, sample RFPs, and other such material.

At Videoplaza, most of our customers had never bought an ad server, let alone known how to migrate to a new one. Doubleclick or whatever homegrown server they had was all they'd ever known. We quickly learned that we'd have to be much more prescriptive in spelling out what they'd need to consider to evaluate a purchase and the process for migrating to another system. This gave new prospects comfort in making the leap to our platform.

Assess sales cycle lengths over time.

Your sales cycle will necessarily be longer at the beginning. You don't have case studies from referenceable customers. You are still figuring your motion out and developing pattern recognition as to what constitutes a well-qualified lead. Over time, you will streamline your process to shorten the sales cycle, unless you move further upmarket.

Remember, however, that each sales motion has a natural asymptote based on the "physics" of the industry. You will experience diminishing returns if you optimize at the asymptote. For instance, if you are selling a new way for trains to navigate, no matter how much you've streamlined your sales process, there's no getting around the fact that procurement cycles are a yearslong process. You're better off focusing on building more pipeline than streamlining your process.

Document.

Last, document, document, document. Develop your sales playbook to memorialize expectations and experience at every step of the process. This will be a living document that will prove invaluable as you build out the go-to-market team. Having training materials for new reps will give leverage and enable them to be productive more quickly. Getting the average rep productive even a month earlier than normal will move the needle on your revenues over time.

Once you've committed to your sales motion, you'll be better placed to determine how to reliably generate demand.

❖❖❖

CHAPTER 7

RELIABLY GENERATE DEMAND

Up until now most of your leads may have come via your network, your university, accelerators, or the like. Repeatable sales require programmatically creating and converting demand. You will need to reliably fill the top of your sales funnel with leads or else be scrambling quarter to quarter as your pipeline thins out. The rule of thumb is to have three times the pipeline to hit your number in a given timeframe. So, you'll need to create at least three dollars of pipeline for every incremental dollar of growth in your plan.

First things first: **commit to a marketing strategy**.

Most B2B startups will adopt one of three marketing strategies:

Account-based marketing (ABM): As the name suggests, ABM involves identifying and focusing on key accounts. It's most relevant when selling into verticals where most of the business is driven by a few accounts. At Videoplaza, we targeted the top broadcasters, publishers, and online video networks, amounting to maybe a dozen or two accounts max in any given country.

Vertical: A vertical strategy requires going deep in the named industry(ies), going to the right trade shows and events, and tying up with trade groups. Market-based insight drives vertical plays, and so it was with Abhishek Jha at Elucidata. Although their cloud data platform could be used in other industries, they are laser-focused on biotech and pharma.

Horizontal: In contrast, a horizontal marketing strategy involves targeting functions that span multiple verticals. For instance, Quala, the customer success platform, targets heads of Customer Success regardless of their vertical.

A hybrid approach can make sense for some in which you have your outbound prospecting efforts focused on named accounts while your marketing efforts target the broader vertical. Each strategy has KPIs to measure success and will inform the tactics you prioritize to achieve it. With myriad marketing tactics, it's important to stack rank these based on the strategy and avoid diluting your limited marketing resources across. The most common tactics for each strategy, as well as the KPIs, are laid out in the following table:

Marketing Strategy Framework	Account-Based Marketing	Vertical	Horizontal
Product-led/ Freemium	N/A	E.g., Vention Thought leadership, SEO	E.g., Airtable Content factory, SEO
Inbound	Thought leadership, highly targeted	E.g., Circle	E.g., HubSpot
Paid Channels	Analysts, PR, trade pubs, events	Analysts, PR, search, trade pubs	Search, social
Outreach	Personalized; industry databases	Industry databases	Data driven: LinkedIn, Zoominfo
KPIs	Engaged accounts	Leads, industry awareness	Leads, functional awareness

For instance, at Videoplaza, our ABM strategy involved using events and, to a lesser degree, trade publications to reach our target accounts. We easily spent the vast majority of our marketing budget in these two categories. On the other hand, a horizontal SaaS platform could adopt a content-heavy inbound marketing strategy as popularized by HubSpot to drive leads over time. Last, while every context is different, in most B2B startups the Sales team generates the vast majority of leads via outbound prospecting early on. As the company grows, marketing takes on more of the load. I'll break the rest of this chapter into two parts then, first covering outbound prospecting and then marketing demand generation, bearing in mind that the tactic should fit your overall strategy.

OUTBOUND PROSPECTING

"CEOs are remarkably accessible and easy to reach... When I was in college in the 1990s, I would send cold emails to people like Steve Jobs, then the CEO of Next, and Steve Ballmer (then #2 at

Microsoft). Both of them would reply within hours...to a college student."[32]

—AUREN HOFFMAN

Whereas you may have been haphazard or meandering in outbound prospecting during the Zero-to-One phase, you'll need to get more systematic about it to scale. That means creating a process comprising target list creation and programmatic outreach.

Target list creation should be based on your segments and buyer personas. There are a number of tools that enable this, such as LinkedIn, Crunchbase, and Zoominfo. Programmatic outreach uses customer relationship management (CRM) and marketing automation tools like HubSpot and Marketo to sequentially reach out, determine who is engaging with your messaging, and easily create meetings.

SALES DEVELOPMENT

Beyond the process itself, at some point you will need to stand up a sales development representative (SDR) function.[33] SDRs are responsible for generating leads via qualifying inbound inquiries and proactive outreach. SDRs build out target lists too via desk research. Some companies choose to outsource SDRs before eventually bringing it in-house. The starting price for either in-house or outsourced is $5,000 per month. The latter have access to tools, databases, and best practices that you

---

32 Auren Hoffman, "How to Write a Great Cold Email That Will Actually Get a Response," *Summation by Auren Hoffman*, May 4, 2020, https://summation.net/2020/05/04/how-to-write-a-great-cold-email-that-will-actually-get-a-response. Well worth a read.

33 This is also called business development representative. These are interchangeable and I'll stick to SDR for consistency.

won't have, but you'll be getting a fraction of a head compared to someone dedicated solely to your goals. Your mileage will vary, but having one SDR for every one to two account executives is typical for companies with less than $10 million ARR.

Prospecting is a team sport.

Don't just rely on SDRs, though. Outbound prospecting is a team sport. You and your reps should regularly block off time to do outreach. One of my portfolio companies has an outreach hour every Tuesday where the founders and field team get together on Zoom to send out emails and make calls to drive meetings. It makes for a shared experience, lessening the monotony of cold outreach and even making it fun. Prospecting responsibility doesn't stop at your sales team or even within your company.

Most startups don't leverage their network of friends and family enough. This includes investors, board members, vendors, bankers, lawyers, industry groups, and university networks. All of these stakeholders have a vested interest in your success and also have networks that trust them to surface relevant technologies. Don't be shy about having them prospect for you. Help them help you by specifying whom they can reach out to and the message.

BREAKING THROUGH THE NOISE

The brute force approach to outreach is increasingly ineffective. Buyers today are bombarded by robo-emailed solicitations. It is far better to customize the message if you want to break through the noise, especially for top-down businesses. This doesn't just mean greeting them by name; indicate some knowledge of their work or priorities to give them a reason to take a meeting.

Being provocative works well, especially at high levels in an organization.

The people you're calling on get constantly pitched and are on a defensive footing. Knocking on these doors can feel like pounding your head against the wall. Try going to the top with a provocative message that might not be what they're used to hearing. Senior management frequently receive distilled reports from their underlings, and so the right executive will be attuned to insights they're not getting from their troops. But strike the right tone so as not to alienate. Try something like this:

> *Dear Julia, we've had a hard time engaging with your automation team. I'm sure they're busy with high priorities but I did want to call something out. We believe Widget Corp's current automation strategy, heavily reliant on Lidar, is deeply flawed. Based on my Ph.D. research and our experience with your peers, a Lidar-reliant strategy won't scale to the use cases we believe you will need to cover and will become a dead end for your efforts. Can we connect for thirty minutes in the coming week so I can brief you further on this?*

This strikes a respectfully provocative tone and connects unique insight into Widget Corp's strategy.

Target one to a few levels down from the C-suite.

Typically, the people owning the budget and having the authority to buy your product will be in middle- to upper-management, but not at the very top and certainly not at the bottom. Think of an operations manager at a warehouse, the head of customer success at a SaaS company, or the head of R & D at a biotech company. They'll have the authority to procure for their division or function but sit a couple of levels down in the organization from the top.

Get creative.

At Live365 during the heyday of the dot-com boom, we found it really hard to get responses to our emails or phone calls to prospective investors or partners. People still had fax machines back then and so we faxed our emails over, with a far higher hit rate than any other medium. Who knew?! In 2021, with so many people working remotely, companies are turning to handwritten notes and thoughtful gifts to get their message out there.

MARKETING DEMAND GENERATION

In addition to building your prospecting muscle, you'll also need to systematically generate demand via marketing activities. These can be abstracted into a three-stage funnel:

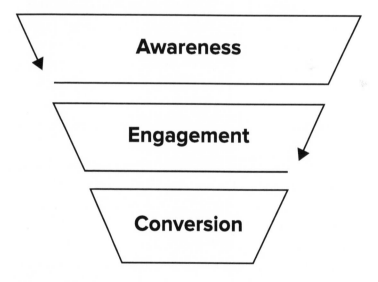

AWARENESS

Awareness has to do with educating potential buyers on their need in the first place. If yours is a breakthrough product or doesn't neatly fit into an existing category, you will probably spend most of your marketing calories in this bucket. KPIs in this category comprise number of mentions and share of voice.[34] Generating awareness requires evangelism and education with the most common tactics comprising the following:

PR and Speaking: Being covered by industry press, writing contributed articles, speaking at industry events, and doing podcasts are all effective ways of broadcasting your message and creating awareness. During the One-to-Ten phase, you'll want to systematize this by hiring either a PR firm or a freelance PR professional. Eventually, your head of marketing will want to bring this function, often called marcom, in-house while also maintaining agency relationships.

A word on using PR agencies and freelance professionals: PR agencies and freelance professionals work on either a fixed project or monthly retainer basis. The latter costs anywhere from $5,000 to $20,000 per month or more depending on the scope. Whichever way you go, bear in mind the following:

- While agencies will help you flesh out various story angles and leverage their media relationships, they are as good as what they have to work with. The media most want to write stories involving customers and business outcomes. You'll waste money and cycles if you don't have enough material for an agency to work with.
- Clarify their objective. Is it to drive awareness in the market and potential customers or in the investment community? These involve different tactics and messaging.
- The best PR professionals will translate what you're doing

---

34 An easy way to calculate SoV is the number of mentions of your brand divided by total number of brand mentions (you and your competitors).

into messaging that resonates with target outlets. They'll feel comfortable challenging you and pushing back. On the other hand, I've had experiences with agencies that just don't get it, where I'm rewriting press releases that they've drafted and every meeting seems like a chore. That's when you know you have the wrong partner.

- Note that agencies will bring in their senior people and tout their media relationships to win your business, but they will seldom be involved in the week-to-week. Instead, get to know the people directly responsible for your account and invest in this relationship as you would a direct report. It will pay dividends in their ability to represent you.

Analysts: Analyst coverage bestows credibility and leads. Founders that ignore analyst relations may be missing a trick. Analysts are always on the lookout for what's next to bring to their corporate clients so they should be receptive to innovators like yourself. Consider commissioning an analyst to write a white paper to be delivered in a webinar or event setting.

Social Media: Communicate your thought leadership via social media channels, but this will require regular upkeep. A master at viral videos showcasing its robot dog technology, Boston Dynamics has nearly 2.5 million subscribers to its YouTube channel, many of whom have no doubt turned into leads for their Spot product.

ENGAGEMENT

Engagement should be the primary focus for companies in established categories where the goal is to route existing category demand your way. Engagement KPIs range from open rate, click-through rate, and monthly visits to touchpoints—for instance, whether a lead downloaded a piece of content. The good news is that you don't have to convince people about the category itself. The bad news is that an established category indicates competition, so you'll need to find ways to stand out from the crowd.

Trade Shows: These investments can range from a tabletop to a full-blown booth and all the trappings. If you don't know an event, it's better to first "walk the show" and invest the following year. There are some industries, however, where you just have to show up. DMEXCO was the premier adtech event in Europe, and Videoplaza just had to be there. On the other hand, I can't remember doing any trade shows at all in my seven years at Brightcove.

Events: Organizing your own events can be one of the highest ROI engagement tactics. It need not be a glitzy, highly produced affair. At Videoplaza, we held customer and prospect dinners for under $1,000, and a daylong customer summit for not much more than that.

Trade Publications: Cultivating relationships with trade pubs yields benefits. They can put together campaigns to drive leads via sponsored articles, webinars, and emails.

Content-driven SEO: Inbound marketing involves a long-term mindset but can be the best, most cost-effective form of lead gen when in a crowded space. According to HubSpot, which literally wrote the book on the subject, "Inbound marketing is a business methodology that attracts customers by creating valuable content and experiences tailored to them."[35] HubSpot

35 "What Is Inbound Marketing?" HubSpot, accessed June 13, 2021, https://www.hubspot.com/inbound-marketing.

scientifically calculates the potential traffic that content can generate based on key phrase matching, then creates an editorial calendar and content that includes these keywords.[36]

Paid Search and Social: At a minimum, invest in purchasing search terms around your brand and your product.

CONVERSION

Conversion has to do with qualifying your lead flow. The more bottom-up products you're offering, the more mature this will need to be. Conversion rates (%) and cost per marketing qualified lead are the most common KPIs here. Tactics to spur conversion include:

Your Web Presence: The user experience on your site—messaging and positioning, product pages, the knowledge base, product videos, case studies, and the call to action—plays a big role in conversion. Other effective tactics in this bucket include having live chat integrated into the site and self-guided product tours.

Email: Email communication remains one of the most effective tactics to nurture and activate those leads that are ready.

BUILDING THE DEMAND-GENERATION ENGINE

Creating demand really means building a machine to test marketing channels and doubling down on the ones that work, until you get diminishing returns to that channel, when you have to find the next one. For startups in the One-to-Ten phase,

---

36   Lenny Rachitsky has good case studies and a framework for content-driven growth, Lenny Rachitsky, "Content-driven growth," *Lenny's Newsletter*, March 2, 2021, https://www.lennysnewsletter.com/p/content-driven-growth-strategy.

it's usually a few channels that work. You will need to determine the best mix across the various channels outlined above, which should be informed by your marketing strategy and sales motion. Spend your marketing calories on these and avoid spreading out the spend like peanut butter. Then, periodically evaluate the mix by measuring the effectiveness of each channel and altering the tactics and/or the proportions accordingly.

Last, hire a head of marketing. Jason Lemkin wrote of hiring his VP of marketing at $20,000 monthly recurring revenue and that it wasn't a week too early:

"One of the starkest differences I see between first-timers in SaaS and second-timers is when they hire their VP of marketing. Second-timers know. They often hire a VP of demand gen marketing even before they have their first paying customers… What I can tell you both mathematically and qualitatively, is that you almost can't hire a VP of marketing too early. But it's very, very easy to make the hire late. It's not quite as terrible as waiting too long for a VP of sales. But it's still a big missed opportunity."[37]

As you're consistently filling your pipeline with quality leads, you'll need to build out your go-to-market team to turn those leads into deals.

---

37   Jason Lemkin, "I Hired My VP of Marketing at $20k MRR. It Wasn't a Week Too Early," SaaStr, January 30, 2021, https://www.saastr.com/i-hired-my-vp-of-marketing-at-20k-mrr-it-wasnt-a-week-too-early.

CHAPTER 8

BUILD YOUR GO-TO-MARKET TEAM

Let's hear again from James Richards, founder of Teleborder: "I thought at the time, if I'm able to close so many doing this part-time, professional salespeople doing nothing but sales should be able to do so much more. I was wrong."

According to James, founders have an unfair advantage over reps. Founders have been living and breathing their business for years. They effortlessly switch contexts and think on the fly. Their founder status unlocks doors out of reach to the lowly, bag-carrying sales rep.

All too true. But, with the right hiring, onboarding, and managing, you can build out a team that can sell without you.

DETERMINE TEAM MAKEUP

First things first, determine the optimal makeup of your go-to-market team. You'll need the following functions covered:

- **Sales:** Involves everything in running a sales process including prospecting, qualification, presentations and pitching, negotiating, and closing.[38] Sales reps are known as account executives (AEs).

- **Customer Success:** Involves being the customer's main point of contact and ensuring that they are getting value out of your solution and that they'll renew. This function will grow in importance over time as you grow your customers and as they grow their business with you.

- **Sales Engineering or Field Application Engineering[39]:** This function gets the technical win straddling by mapping the customer's requirements to your technology. It can involve giving demos, writing technical proposals, pricing out installations, and doing site visits. The more complex your product, the more you'll need this function as opposed to bottom-up, product-led SaaS companies that may have roles such as product advocates or developer evangelists to advise the customer.

- **Delivery or Professional Services:** These (usually billable) functions architect and implement your solution including provisioning, installation, training, and customization work. As with sales engineering, the more complex your product, the more you'll need to build out this capability.

- **Sales Operations:** Sales ops, sometimes known as business ops or revenue ops, sits between finance and sales and provides leverage to both. Sales ops manages the CRM, optimizes workflows, performs sales analytics, and supports reps from onboarding to pricing to calculating commissions. Your head of sales ought to push for this hire when you have more than a handful of quota-carrying heads.

---

38   Government sales tend to combine pre- and post-sales into one team.

39   These terms are interchangeable and often get lumped into the "pre-sales" bucket.

PRIORITIZING GO-TO-MARKET HIRES

Your team has likely been wearing multiple hats when signing, onboarding, and managing your early customers. How should you prioritize your go-to-market hires? It depends on your stage and your sales motion. You'll need to specialize and build out both pre-sales and post-sales functions. Do not skimp on your post-sale customer experience. It will come back to bite you.

First things first, map out the jobs to be done across the customer lifecycle from pre-sales to renewal. It might look like the following:

Pre-Sales	Onboarding	Customer Value	Transactions
Sourcing	Provisioning	Single point of contact	Up-sell
Qualification	Training		Cross-sell
Technical win	Billing information	Adoption/ Optimization	Renewal
Negotiation	Custom work	Customer advocacy	
Closing	API integration	Ad-hoc tech support	

Once you've identified the jobs to be done, calibrate the need for customer continuity to understand how easily you can specialize your functions. One end of the spectrum would be a business selling a commodity, easy-to-deploy products like Dropbox. There isn't the need for much continuity. As a customer, while you'd have dealt with the Dropbox rep to cut the deal, you're perfectly fine dealing with someone else on an ongoing basis. As a result, a company like Dropbox will have specialized teams dealing with onboarding, billing, tech support, and even renewals.

Videoplaza was at the other end of the spectrum. Our large broadcaster customers expected continuity in the relationship. We could centralize certain functions like billing, but the customers needed their main points of contact to be familiar with the account setup and workflows on an ongoing basis, and so our post-sales teams consisted of account managers and technical account managers. **Higher complexity of product, business model, or deployment requires more continuity with customers. Staff accordingly.**

Based on the jobs to be done, mapping, and continuity, determine the best groupings and roles. For instance, at one portfolio company, it looked like this at the time of their seed round. They are now in the process of creating a Customer Success function to handle onboarding, adoption, and transactions.

Before

Pre-Sales	Onboarding	Customer Value	Business Value
Sourcing	Provisioning	Single Point of Contact	Upsell
Qualification	Training	Adoption/ Optimization	Expansion Revenue
Tech Win	Integration	Customer Advocacy	Renewal
Negotiation	Project Management	Ad Hoc Tech Support	Cross-Sell
Closing	Custom Work		

→ **Engineering**

↑ **Sales**

After

Pre-Sales	Onboarding	Customer Value	Business Value
Sourcing	Provisioning	Single Point of Contact	Upsell
Qualification	Training	Adoption/ Optimization	Expansion Revenue
Tech Win		Customer Advocacy	Renewal
Negotiation	Project Management	Ad Hoc Tech Support	Cross-Sell
Closing	Custom Work		
	Integration		

↑ **Sales**

→ **Professional Services**

↑ **Customer Succces**

Inflections in product standardization and growth will drive future groupings. For instance, the first few deployments of a robot may take heavy lifting. Over time, this will get standardized to the extent that you won't need the same team pre-sales to do the post-sales implementation. You can then plot your go-to-market functions based on business versus technical skills and level of continuity as per the following diagram to understand current and future gaps to be filled.

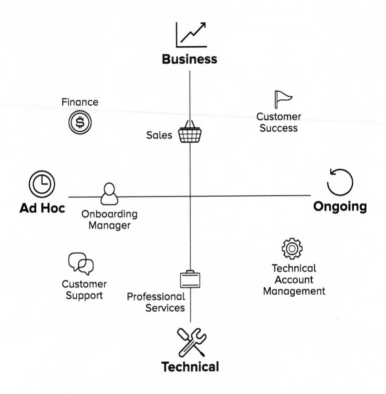

For instance, as your product standardizes and your sales velocity increases, it may make sense to stand up a specialist function to only do onboarding and training.

Prioritize your go-to-market hires on where you get the most leverage.

If you shine on the technical front, then hiring an AE to run sales processes can give you the most leverage. On the other hand, if you're better at evangelizing and telling your story, then hiring a sales engineer to do demos and site visits will likely give you the most leverage. For inside-sales-based sales motions, hiring a customer success manager (CSM) first often makes the most sense. You want someone managing your first customers and ensuring they get value as you're signing more up.

In general, make your first go-to-market hire a sales engineer for highly technical sales, and either a CSM or AE for less technical sales.

Even if you start off with a CSM or SE, you will inevitably need to hire AEs to bring in new accounts. I'll spend most of the rest of this chapter focusing on hiring and managing AEs. It's where technical founders have the most trouble.

HIRING SALES REPS

Hiring AEs is risky. Make a mistake in the hire and you've wasted not just significant time and money in paying and ramping them, but also the opportunity cost in losing deals you should have won that may take years to win, if ever.

The first step in hiring the right AEs is to determine how many you need. To do this, work backward from your plan, making reasonable assumptions on quota and achievement. Quota will vary based on industry, product maturity, and business model. There's plenty of data online to help you calibrate. Assume 70 to 80 percent average quota achievement in your modeling.

Next, decide whether you need an individual contributor or a player/coach. The former should be out there hunting new accounts. The latter will have the aptitude and aspiration to be a manager and be able to build out the function. Importantly, they should be willing to roll up their sleeves and run their own deals. What you don't want is a pure manager just yet.

No matter which you choose, make sure that you hire experienced AEs. A director-level AE will be the default for most startups at the beginning of their journey from One to Ten. You'll want someone with sales experience who can get deals done. Hiring junior AEs with no sales manager is too risky and may not give you the leverage you need.

THE SPECTRUM OF ACCOUNT EXECUTIVES

Sales reps come in various flavors along a spectrum. At one end is what we'll call "market-making," at the other end "coin-operated," with points in between.

Just as it sounds, market-making AEs make their own market. They evangelize your vision, networking into accounts without a lot of support and finding deals. During this journey, they are helping you build your playbook. They may also have a small rogue streak, not always following a script or method. That's to be expected. After all, they are mini entrepreneurs for their market and will need to be creative and courageous to plant your flag.

On the other hand, you may encounter coin-operated AEs. Feed him (and this is predominantly a male type) leads; equip with scripts, a deck, and other materials; and watch him go. Coin-operated reps are machines, running the playbook over and over. They thrive on structure and are highly process-driven. Beware of changing the playbook or deploying them to situations requiring market-making skills.

Bias toward market-making AEs early on when you're proving the ability to go beyond founder selling.

Hire coin-operated AEs when you reach repeatability in your sales process. In fact, your eventual VP of sales should be the one hiring coin-operated AEs, so I'll focus on market-making AEs for the rest of this chapter.

There are various AE archetypes that you'll encounter:

- **The Rolodex:** This rep relies on the network they've built up in the years, or even decades, that they've been in the domain. They can be effective when using this network to open doors, especially getting high-level access when you otherwise couldn't. Probe for culture fit and whether this rep is willing to roll up their sleeves. While these reps can be effective, they can also use their network as leverage to do things their own way. A big red flag is if an AE keeps their contacts to themselves.
- **The Newly Minted MBA Grad:** New grads from a respected MBA program can be effective market-making reps. They are hungry to prove themselves, are able to network, can think on their feet, and like the idea of helping create the sales playbook. On the other hand, pitfalls with this profile are around the grad either having mismatched expectations (i.e., they want to be CEO within a year) or else not being able to close deals.
- **The Up-and-Comer:** This person may have started in an SDR role and is looking for their next step up. They're hungry, a quick study, and have already gotten the taste of sales. I'm a big fan of this profile. They won't have the network, but having ambition and hustle will go a long way as an individual contributor.

- **The Partner Manager:** This person has worked as a relationship manager or in a business development (BD) capacity at other companies. They are great with relationships, but when you probe further you discover they can't actually close. These people may be best to manage large accounts one day, but avoid them at the early stages.
- **The Midcareer Professional:** They've been working in quota-carrying roles for several years and are wanting to take the next step in their career. These make good candidates for early sales hires as a player/coach. Their growth opportunity is to help write the playbook and potentially manage a team.

HOW TO HIRE YOUR MARKET-MAKING ACCOUNT EXECUTIVES

What to look for when hiring market-making AEs? First, be thoughtful about the qualities you value the most.[40] While every company and culture are different, I look for certain attributes when recruiting market-making reps. This list comes later, but first, let me tell you a story about hiring an admin assistant who happened to have these traits.

Spring 2006.

My boss at Brightcove, Elisabeth Bentel Carpenter, was hiring an administrative assistant for herself and our team. It was down to two people. The first, we'll call her Jen, had been an assistant at other companies and seemed nice and competent. The other, Kash Razzaghi, was an electrical engineering grad out of Mississippi State who had started a custom apparel business

---

40 Mark Roberge, in his excellent book *The Sales Acceleration Formula*, outlines the qualities they valued the most at HubSpot, which has informed my thinking. Recommended.

while at school. I have no idea how he made it up to Boston or got in for an interview, but here he was.

It wasn't even close.

I went into Elisabeth's office and gave her my take: "Jen will be fine. She's done it before and seems personable. But I vote for Kash. He's got this fire in his belly and a look in his eye. The only flag is that he won't be in the role very long." I added, with a laugh, "In fact, he's going to be running this shop one day."

I was right.[41] Kash stayed for six years, getting into sales within a couple of quarters of being hired. In Kash's words: "I figured I would learn a lot if I could shadow an executive and watch how they operate as their assistant. Yes, you'd do mundane work, but I'd learn through osmosis…I was in an office with sales reps and listened to them all day. After a few months, I figured I could do the job. So, when a sales rep position opened up, I put a presentation together. I'll never forget it. One Friday afternoon, I caught Elisabeth before she left the office and pitched her on giving me the role even though I had zero tech sales experience. She said she'd think about it, and I got the job that next week."

Fast-forward to 2018 when Kash rejoined Brightcove as SVP of Sales for the Americas. He was running the shop.

TRAITS OF A MARKET-MAKING AE

The traits that Kash displayed were obvious. The right market-making AEs for your team should be just as clear. Here are some

---

41   He had all the attributes that you'll find below, and then some.

traits to look out for as you move through your interviewing process.

- **Entrepreneurship and evangelism.** Have they shown an entrepreneurial spirit in other endeavors? Could they be your clone and sell the vision to customers without you there? Maybe they have a side hustle. Evidence of their having created a new book of business for a past employer is a great signal. Probe as to how they did this, what support they received, and what they did themselves.
- **Adaptability.** Ensure they have the mental agility and emotional maturity to be able to adapt to a changing context and pivot to a different playbook.
- **Coachability.** Reps need to be open to taking feedback and changing tacks.
- **Intelligence.** Market-making reps, especially those not from the domain, will have the intellectual horsepower to come up to speed on new terminology and markets and see patterns.
- **Technical prowess.** While you'll augment the AE with sales engineering, they still need to have enough of a grasp on your technology to be credible to the customer.
- **Competitiveness.** Do they have the hunger and ambition to compete? How have they successfully competed in the past? Look for a fire in the belly.
- **Closing.** Last, look for evidence that they're able to actually negotiate and close deals.

INTERVIEWING AND OTHER CONSIDERATIONS

Salespeople thrive on making connections and talking a good game, so it can be tough to parse the good fits from those that aren't, especially if you are mainly used to dealing with engineers. Use the following interview techniques.

Have them walk you through a deal they've done that would be most representative of your own sales motion.

Get into the "forensics" of the deal. Keep probing along each step so you really understand what role they played versus the rest of their team. Did they go out and source the prospect or was it handed to them? Who filled out the proposal? What involvement did the founders have? Why did the customer buy?

Ask them for a relevant accomplishment of theirs that would point to future success in this role.

Test their understanding of your context and their self-awareness. Do they point to something truly similar or does their example belie a blind spot? For instance, they could point to a growth situation at another company but one where they came in later and were given a playbook to execute.

Ask them to tell you about a deal they lost.

What I look for here is whether they ran the right process and what they learned from it. Do they take accountability, or do they point the finger at the product, their boss, the customer, everyone but themselves? Bad answers involve not taking accountability, not showing learning, or lazy answers like "I lost it on price."

Ask for specific examples of feedback they took on board and how it panned out.

Their ability to be coached is paramount for your transition phase. If they don't have examples of being coached, or don't show an aptitude for responding to feedback, they will likely become a roadblock in the future.

Pay attention to how they run the process with you.

Are they continuously qualifying the fit? Are they listening properly and using this information in your interactions? Are they always closing, asking for feedback, and discussing next steps before the end of a meeting? Are they persistent without being annoying? Are they responsive or lax in their follow-up?

Have them give a pitch.

I give them the choice of either presenting something they already know or, as a greater challenge, putting a pitch together based on their knowledge of our product. The bar is lower for the latter since they don't have all the context, but great candidates will impress by synthesizing their research into a cogent pitch. This approach works for SEs, FAEs, and marketing hires as well. You want to experience how the candidate carries themselves in front of the customer. Are they quick on their feet or do they get flustered? Do they listen to questions or speak over them? Can you imagine them representing you and your company without you being there?

Don't over-index on domain experience and Rolodex.

Having a Rolodex is helpful but also overrated. A good AE will be able to network their way into prospects. Sure, they'll need help at first, but within a year they should be able to build relationships in the domain. One of my companies was selling into an insular vertical with no prior knowledge or many relationships save for one key advisor who sponsored them into some key accounts. Within twelve months, they were well-known in the vertical, landing deals and building pipeline. All with no reps from the domain.

Beware of candidates from the domain with no sales experience.

One of my advisee companies, with a highly technical buyer persona, tried a candidate who used to be a scientist themselves. But while the rep could speak the language, they couldn't run sales processes or close. The hire didn't work out.

Sales experience at large incumbents is very different than in smaller players or startups. Bias toward the latter.

Hiring someone from a gorilla in the space may seem attractive. They have a Rolodex and know the domain. But many of these AEs struggle to transition to a startup. They're used to the established processes and infrastructure of the mother ship, from the deal desk to the army of sales engineers to write proposals to the corporate expense account to wine and dine customers. By definition, many of these reps tend to be coin-operated.

Consultants and agents can be effective IF properly managed.

Not every revenue-generating head need be full-time. Sometimes the market doesn't justify it. That's where consultants and agents can be effective to open doors, build relationships, and generate pipeline. They're especially effective when you need presence in a market. For instance, at one startup, we felt it important to have someone in Silicon Valley to do impromptu meetings and so we had a part-time consultant to be our West

Coast presence. He had a company email address and internal access, but he was on a retainer to work one or two days per week with commission on deals.

The key is to manage them like they're part of your team, with training, onboarding, and setting clear expectations—for instance, do you want them to mainly network and open doors or do you expect them to run the entire sales process?

ONBOARDING ACCOUNT EXECUTIVES

Once you've identified the right AEs for your goals, it's time to properly onboard them to your team. Do not take a haphazard approach to onboarding AEs. The longer it takes to onboard an AE, the longer they take to be productive, shortening your runway. Cutting down an AE's ramp from three months to two can be material for your business at scale. That said, if they aren't given the best documentation and training, their meetings won't produce the results you need to grow. Find the right balance between support and holding them back.

Develop an onboarding plan and bias toward spending more time with the rep at the beginning. Give them quick feedback, ideally immediately after a sales call or meeting. Gauge if they incorporate this in your subsequent interactions. Optimize for the following milestones, understanding that mileage will vary depending on your product, your market, and the rep themselves.

- **Leading a presentation and demo.** At first, invite them along to sales calls as a fly on the wall. Soon thereafter, throw them in the deep end by having them lead their first pitch. This is a great forcing function for them. After this, the next milestone is their being able to do meetings without you feeling like you need to be there. This will unlock all kinds of leverage for yourself.

- **Putting a proposal together.** Review what they've written and make sure you're happy with the work product.
- **Closing their first deal.** This should happen as quickly as possible even if it requires you to help more than you feel you need to. Getting the first win, even if you teed it up well, will increase their confidence and their standing internally.

Build in enough onboarding buffer.

Remember James Richards, the founder of Teleborder? One of his biggest mistakes was assuming that new reps would ramp more quickly than they did. While high-velocity sales AEs can be productive on the order of weeks, enterprise reps can take up to four quarters to start hitting quota, depending on the sales cycle and product complexity. Be sure they're set up for success by having aggressive but realistic expectations on ramp.

Set them up for success with the right tools.

Just like engineers need to be equipped with the right tools, so it goes with AEs and your go-to-market team. At minimum, AEs should have a CRM system and sales materials. Beyond these basics, there may be a need for other tools for prospecting (LinkedIn, Crunchbase), presentations (Loom, Zoom), and customer data.

DESIGNING SALES COMP PLANS

Sales and BD professionals have variable compensation, usually commissions based on their sales, as a significant part of their on-target earnings (OTE). View variable comp as a tool to incent performance and drive behavior.

THE WELL-CONSTRUCTED PLAN

First, decide if you'll have variable compensation at all. There is a school of thought that eschews sales commissions for salary and ties all employees into the same bonus and equity structure instead of having a separate plan for quota-carrying reps.[42] These companies contend that commission plans drive the wrong behavior internally and with customers, resulting in higher staff turnover and even a toxic culture. These are valid concerns, although not having the ability to overachieve and get large commission checks may impact your ability to hire the best reps. At any rate, the vast majority of enterprise companies continue to have variable comp. Let's assume this will be the case for you.

Next, determine what portion of overall earnings variable comp should be. The less mature the product and sales process, the smaller variable comp should be as a percent of the overall. Otherwise it's not fair to the rep, and you don't want them chasing the wrong things. Whereas you may have gone with a straight salary or management by objectives (MBO)-based bonus for a BD person during the Zero-to-One phase, variable should be a significant portion of on-target compensation during the One-to-Ten phase. While mileage will vary based on product maturity and market, variable comp should comprise 20 to 50 percent of overall on-target earnings.

Finally, clarify the principles behind your plan. Sales targets

42   Doug J. Chung, "How to Really Motivate Salespeople," *Harvard Business Review*, April 2015, https://hbr. org/2015/04/how-to-really-motivate-salespeople.

must align to company objectives or they will drive the wrong behavior. The targets should be ambitious but reachable and the plan payouts should be motivating to the rep, or else it will be worse than having no plan at all. There is always a trade-off between having a sales comp plan reflect your company's priorities and complexity. Bias toward simplicity.

For instance, you may wish to only pay out after a certain threshold is met, to incent deals with upfront payments and multiyear terms, and to protect yourself from customers that don't pay. All well and good, but you are adding complexity to the plan. Complex plans are best for larger, more mature companies.

Avoid legislating for every scenario. Corner cases will arise. It's hard to anticipate all these scenarios in a simple comp plan. Both parties just have to take a leap of faith and trust in the other to be fair. You do need to decide if there's a minimum percent achievement that they need to hit before getting paid out as well as if there's an accelerator for overachievement. Those details should be clear from the beginning. In addition, do you have separate commission rates for services bookings and product bookings due to the different margins? Bias toward simplicity and err on the side of paying out too much rather than too little. You can always change the plan in a future period.

A well-constructed plan is one where you'll be thrilled to make large payouts. Remember, sales comp is a tool to achieve outcomes. No one benefits from a plan that's too hard to hit or too complicated to understand. Even worse, it will demoralize the sales team. As you construct your plan, model various scenarios and the ensuing payouts. How happy would your future self be in each case?

QUOTAS AND TARGETS

These will obviously depend on your context, your sales motion, and product maturity. Before achieving product–market fit, comping reps aside from bookings makes sense. For instance, landing a referenceable logo will add a ton of value and the rep should be comped accordingly. On the other hand, once you have product readiness, sales reps should have commissions based on quotas. A few points to remember about quotas and targets:

- Most quotas tend to be quarterly to ensure accountability. When you have a long sales cycle, an annual quota can also work as long as there are milestones along the way for accountability.
- Quotas are a function of deal size and velocity.
- Outside enterprise reps selling SaaS software have a median quota of $1 million in ARR (with nonrecurring revenue being separate from this), whereas the 50th percentile for inside reps is at $500,000. You'll need to prorate quotas based on when a rep joins and ramps as well.
- Quotas involving hardware that's purchased on a capex basis should be higher, perhaps 33 to 50 percent, than pure software ones.
- Set quotas that are ambitious but achievable. It's demoralizing for reps to have a target that they have no chance of hitting.
- Quota attainment: not every rep hits their quota. In fact, if they do, you've probably set your quotas too low. Eighty to ninety percent attainment across all reps is healthy and is borne out by the Redpoint 2020 GTM Survey.[43]
- Quota coverage: set quotas such that they sum to 10 to 20

---

43   Tomasz Tunguz, "Top 10 Learnings from the Redpoint 2020 GTM Survey," June 25, 2020, https://tomtunguz.com/redpoint-2020-gtm-survey.

percent more than your overall bookings goal. This is called quota coverage. So, if you have a bookings goal of $4 million, you'll want the combination of reps and quotas to sum to $4.4 to $4.8 million for sufficient coverage.

With your AEs hired and onboarded, time to focus elsewhere, right? Not so much. You need to manage your AEs, even the most ambitious, self-sufficient ones. Let's talk about the best ways to manage sales reps for someone who's never managed any.

MANAGING ACCOUNT EXECUTIVES

Managing sales reps can be tricky for technical founders. Their job is to sell, and that can mean selling you on how good their pipeline is looking. Use the following principles when managing reps.

Put in place a weekly pipeline meeting and weekly or biweekly 1:1s.

Pipeline meetings involve all reps as well as other stakeholders such as Product and Pre-Sales. The goal is to understand the state of the overall pipeline and discuss top deals to provide transparency and identify where cross-functional help may be needed.

Augment pipeline meetings with weekly or biweekly 1:1 meetings with your AEs to take a deeper dive into their activities. Reps tend to gloss over bad news or inconvenient truths. Watch out for these and probe deeper. However, this is not meant to be a time to trap your team. Rather, this should be a candid discussion of where things stand and where the risks are.

For instance, let's say there's a deal in advanced stages where, in all honesty, the rep doesn't really have a feel for what the customer's driving urgency is. That's okay. Brainstorm ways that you could uncover this information and know that the deal may not be one to count on when it comes to forecasting.

Also, ask AEs to write call reports and share them with cross-functional shareholders. They're a great way to share what's happening in the field and will also force the AE to take a step back and process what they heard and how the process is playing out.

See them in action and give prompt feedback.

Whether it's accompanying them in meetings or listening into calls, you want to evaluate how they're qualifying, how they're pitching your vision and value proposition. Provide feedback immediately after and reinforce during your 1:1 if needed. The newer the rep, the more time you'll want to spend with them.

Review and critique their written artifacts, too, such as emails and proposals. I've hired some reps who have been effective verbal communicators but poor at writing. Poorly written proposals don't reflect well on your company and you'll want to support them with templates and scripts.

Use a checklist when evaluating deals.

There are a number of sales frameworks such as Value Selling,[44] Miller Heiman, Challenger, and Solution Selling, each of which has a shared vocabulary to discuss deals. You'll want to adopt a framework, ideally driven by your VP of sales. If you're not

---

44   I used Value Selling at Ooyala among others. It works well for complex enterprise sales motions.

sure which framework to use, compile a checklist that will break down the major items when qualifying a deal or start with the classic BANT (budget, authority, need, and timing).

Let market-making reps play a hunch from time to time.

There will be times when a rep wants to push a deal forward that doesn't check the boxes, that others don't believe in. But they have a hunch, some innate sense that it's worth pursuing. Let them explore the hunch, within reason. I've learned that these hunches can pay off even if, at the time, it's not really rational to pursue the deal.

We had this play out at Videoplaza with a rep named Xavi.[45] He wanted to pursue what we thought was a pipe dream—to form a quasi-joint venture (JV) with the two major Spanish broadcasters for their remnant digital video inventory. It didn't make sense on paper, nor did it make sense when Xavi, a fast-talking Catalan with a heavy accent, explained it to us. But we'd made little progress in our direct discussions with the broadcasters, so I let Xavi run with it. A couple of quarters later, he made it happen. We did the JV, which was then a stepping stone to working directly with the two broadcasters. It was a brilliant move that looked irrational at the time.

TROUBLESHOOTING AE PERFORMANCE

There will be instances in which your AEs will not perform to your expectations. The root cause of this gap could be any number of things, but no matter what it is, don't ignore it expecting it to resolve itself. Face the problems head-on and

---

45   A true market-making rep!

as soon as possible. Here are a few strategies for getting to the core issues and fixing them with your AEs.

Expectations: Start with expectations. Are they realistic? Did you expect the rep to be hitting quota within a quarter when you have a much longer sales cycle? Are they up against an entrenched incumbent in an insular market? Do they have sufficient tools and a mature enough product to be able to be effective? Calibrate expectations if needed.

Outbound Prospecting: The AE can run with an existing process but has trouble penetrating new accounts. This usually comes down to either confidence and credibility, or mentality.

In the former, the rep is trying outreach but doesn't have a calling card that gives them the credibility to have their calls returned. The fix here is for them to dive even deeper into the industry, trade articles, papers, whatever it takes to get more up to speed and start developing perspectives that customers will find valuable.

Otherwise, it's likely the rep's mentality. The rep actually doesn't enjoy hunting out new leads. They feel uncomfortable cold emailing or calling people, or even tracking them down at a conference.

All AEs should regularly carve out time, ideally on a weekly basis, for outbound prospecting. One effective tactic is to periodically conduct outbound "jam sessions." Block off a half day and get yourself, the AE, and any other relevant people together in the same room (or Zoom room as the case may be). Everybody gets assigned a list of prospects to call and a script, typically focused around setting an appointment. And then start working the phones, emails, and other channels. There's an energy that people feed off of from being in the trenches with their colleagues, celebrating good calls, laughing off bad ones.

Pitching and Process: The rep isn't convincing when pitching your solution. You can tell by the body language and tone of the customer. It's important to unpack this further and understand where they're falling down. In one of my portfolio companies, it turns out that the founder and product team had built a data platform for end-to-end usage whereas the rep was mostly focused on selling a point solution. Often the root cause comes down to a disconnect in product marketing. Conduct role-play sessions with your reps and give constructive feedback to one another.

Inability to Close: The rep can get into accounts and run processes with little to show. Their deals keep stalling if not being lost altogether. This is the toughest situation because the seemingly sound inputs don't match with the outputs. These boil down to three root causes:

- **Qualification.** The rep isn't actually covering their bases when running the process and isn't qualifying out enough, so their pipeline looks better than it actually is, which you'll see reflected in the win rate. Revisit qualification criteria and challenge them to qualify out more often. It may be that your product lacks key table stakes features but you are still pursuing the deals. Again, you should be qualifying out and/or ensuring product readiness before making a run at these.
- **Killer instinct.** Sometimes, they just lack that killer instinct to go for the close and not let go. They are too passive. Try to coach this but it's hard. If they can't get there, consider moving them to a CS role or else parting ways.

- **Bad luck.** Reps can have bad quarters and can bounce back after coaching, or just plain bad luck. I've had them myself when I was carrying a bag. But bad luck isn't persistent so this should only hold for a quarter or two.

Most managers wait too long to part ways with underperforming AEs. I'm guilty of this as well. Look for signs of improvement. If the inputs are improving, then the output will follow suit. But make the tough choice to terminate a rep if their behaviors aren't improving or fitting your sales motion. It's worse to carry an unproductive rep who doesn't properly represent you.

HIRING YOUR FIRST SALES MANAGER

At some point, you're going to need a single person to manage your entire sales team. Building a repeatable sales machine entails hiring your first head of sales. There are two paths to doing this.

TWO HIRING PATHS
1. Individual Contributors → Manager

This path involves you hiring and managing the first two or three individual contributor AEs.

They should get you to your first $2 to $5 million in ARR. Once you get them productive, you promote one or bring someone in as the head of sales.

2. Business Partner → Individual Contributors → Manager

In this approach, you partner with someone more senior, relying on them to be a player/coach to get deals done while hiring reps and, eventually, a VP of sales. While the title of this person can vary—president, COO, CRO, even CEO—fundamentally you view them as a "business co-founder" or partner while you focus on product and engineering. You'll pay more in equity and compensation, but the upside can be huge if you gear toward your respective strengths and have the right chemistry.

WHAT TO LOOK FOR IN A HEAD OF SALES

Look for candidates with track records in:

- Recruiting and managing well-executing sales teams. How do they hire and onboard new reps? How have they handled underperforming reps?
- Delivering consistent results. Get specific with numbers and how they achieved them. Dive into a year or quarter when they fell short of plan to understand why they missed and what they learned from it.
- Putting sales infrastructure into place. Whether it's sales tools, sales methodology, or building out functions like sales ops and SDR, a VP of sales should be well versed in these various levers for themselves and their team.

Tomasz Tunguz covers the topic further as part of an interview with Mark Roberge:

> Mark shared his three top questions he advises founders to ask head of sales candidates during the recruitment process. They are:
>
> 1. Knowing what you do about our business, what kind of sales methodology would you run? And how does that compare to your previous role? What are the differences between your previous company and this one?

2. What kind of salespeople would you hire, and how do they differ from the people you have hired in the past?

3. How would you structure the compensation plan to meet the needs of our business?

When interviewing head of sales candidates, founders should have decided the kind of sales model they would like to exploit, whether inside sales, field sales, freemium, or channel—or some combination. During the interview process, they should explain to candidates the nuances of their sales processes to better understand how candidates would adapt the processes they know to the uniquenesses of this particular business.

In these interviews, founders and board members should determine whether or not a candidate can combine what they have learned to previous roles, and the new information about this particular company, to forge an alloyed go-to-market strategy that serves this business well. The right candidate needs to be an alchemist, someone who is willing to experiment and tinker with the model, not just copy a previous model by rote.[46]

CUSTOMER SUCCESS

While you'll be focusing on landing new logos, over time you'll want to retain and grow these accounts—acquiring new customers can be five to twenty-five times more expensive than retaining existing ones.[47] That's what Customer Success does. As your recurring revenue base grows, so will the impact of CS, as the percentage of revenue from upsells and renewals will far

---

46 Tomasz Tunguz, "The Three Questions to Ask When Hiring Your Startup's Head of Sales," December 15, 2020, https://tomtunguz.com/three-questions-head-of-sales.

47 Amy Gallo, "The Value of Keeping the Right Customers," *Harvard Business Review*, October 29, 2014, https://hbr.org/2014/10/the-value-of-keeping-the-right-customers.

outweigh that from new customers. In fact, 30 to 40 percent of new bookings should come from upselling existing customers. Following are some best practices on hiring and how to view CS.

SCOPE OF CUSTOMER SUCCESS

Customer Success acts as the single point of contact for a set of accounts; the number of accounts varies based on complexity. At Videoplaza, we had one person solely responsible for our largest account, RTL Germany. On the other hand, product-led, high-velocity ventures can have one customer success manager (CSM) with dozens to hundreds of accounts. Each CSM ought to be able to handle $1 million to $5 million in ARR. I'll focus on CSM activities for top-down, high-value accounts:

- The CSM should be responsible for knowing the account, the customer's objectives, and how your product can help. They champion the account internally while advocating for your company with the customer. They should maintain an account plan that is regularly updated and shared with internal stakeholders.
- The CSM should organize quarterly business reviews (QBRs) with top customers, taking pains to reiterate the value case, i.e., the reasons that the customer decided to work with you. This becomes the North Star for the account and is critical when addressing the inevitable bumps in the road that both parties will face.
- The CSM is usually responsible for onboarding the account if it's a pure SaaS product and driving product usage. For more involved deployments, Professional Services or Operations groups typically quarterback projects that may involve custom development, integration, and training before handing the account off to the CSM when they've gone live.

- The CSM ultimately ensures that the customer is getting value out of your product and aligning economics. CSM best practice involves a proactive stance to engage with customers versus reactively responding to requests or firefighting.
- Less-technical businesses should have the CSM be responsible for most upsell, renewal, and downgrade transactions except when the nature of the transaction is more complex than the CSM can handle. For instance, if there's an opportunity to cross-sell to another division at the customer, it's really a sales opportunity and should be treated as such. For highly technical products or where the CSM has a very large book of business, you're likely better off having an account manager involved to enable the CSM to focus on product adoption and growth.
- However you play it, clearly delineate the roles and responsibilities of CSMs and how they'll be measured, which should include leading indicators of your business and reflect what they have ownership over. These can comprise gross or net dollar retention (as a percentage),[48] customer health score, or number of integrations.
- Last, ensure that your CSMs have the right tools and platforms to be successful. A category called customer success platform (CSP) has emerged this past decade to be to CS what CRMs are for sales and systems like Jira are for engineers.[49] Whatever you choose, there should be a single source of truth for customer engagement and health with clear tasking for the CSM.

Avoid the mistake of not having CSMs responsible for transactions or being too support-focused.

---

48   Sammy Abdullah, "Net vs gross dollar retention stats," Blossom Street Ventures, June 24, 2019, https://blossomstreetventures.com/2019/06/24/net-vs-gross-dollar-retention-stats.

49   Quala is a promising next-gen CSP in which I'm a proud investor.

At one company, the belief was that CSMs would only be responsible for adoption and customer happiness while handing off the "dirty" business of renewals and upsells into the grubby hands of sales. The thinking was that it would be hard to be aligned to the customer's interests while optimizing those of the company. This is a false dichotomy.

This led to Customer Success improperly being viewed as "ticket" chasers within the org. Even worse, it made it hard to pin a value on the function; they couldn't tie retention to CSMs and so they were viewed as a cost center. There was once a budget meeting where the CEO nixed hiring more CSMs, not knowing how they moved the needle. On the other hand, CSMs carried a lot of weight at Videoplaza.[50] They would negotiate renewals and quarterback the accounts.

HIRING CSMS

As Director of Customer Success at HubSpot, with a team of eighty, Celine Kimberly knows a thing or two about CS. Here's how she approaches hiring CSMs:

> Your CSM profile will vary depending on the model you've adopted, the complexity of your product, and the size of the customers you serve. If the industry you operate in or your product is very technical, you should consider hiring someone who's operated in the industry (and can therefore empathize deeply with your customers) or someone who has CSM experience already and can therefore manage multiple stakeholders or coordinate large projects. If you're serving a large volume of relatively small customers and your CSMs carry most of the post-sales jobs to

---

50 We called them account managers at the time but their role was similar, i.e., to be the customer's single point of contact post-sale.

be done, you'll be better off with someone who can prioritize ruthlessly and scale their activities.

At HubSpot, the role of the CSM is to help customers unlock business value and achieve their business outcomes. They do this by driving product adoption and utilization as well as driving growth by exposing customers to new tools. We believe that most CSM skills can be taught "on the job" but we test for key attributes that are hard to coach—for example, the traits we admire that spell HEART[51] (humble, empathetic, adaptable, remarkable, transparent), customer first, curiosity, communication, ownership, organization, self-awareness, and drive for results.

Let's take "drive for results" as an example. A strongly qualified candidate will always perform above their role's expectations. They not only know their customer's goals, but they help uncover new ones to drive better results. Finally, they provide examples of moving complex scenarios in a highly autonomous fashion. To evaluate this attribute, you could ask, "Tell me about a time when you went beyond your manager's expectations to get your job done" or "What are you doing to improve your overall effectiveness at work?"

As you build your post-sales model, start with the competencies you'll need your CSMs to display to successfully manage your customers. Divide the list into must-haves and "coachable." The list of must-haves should be the ones you prioritize during hiring, and you should create three or four questions for each attribute.

As you build out a go-to-market team and onboard them, the

51   "The HubSpot Culture Code," HubSpot, accessed June 13, 2021, https://network.hubspot.com/slides/the-hubspot-culture-code.

focus should shift toward sales execution. I'll cover sales execution in the following chapters, broken down by running quality processes, negotiating win-win deals, and reliably closing deals.

CHAPTER 9

RUN QUALITY SALES PROCESSES

"There are only two reasons you ever lose a deal. Anyone know what those are?"

It was my first ever formal sales training. I didn't want to be there. What did I need to learn in selling? I was already one of Brightcove's best reps. My ears perked up when I heard the instructor ask the question.

The only two reasons to lose a deal are you didn't qualify out, or else you got outsold.

The point: you should be constantly qualifying the fit with the customer. And if the fit is there but the customer chooses another option, you either missed something in qualification or didn't properly position your solution or couldn't negotiate the right deal. In other words, you got outsold.

Many people think sales is all about giving a killer pitch and seeing who bites. Not so. That's called throwing shit at the wall and seeing what sticks. Instead, you need to get good at sales execution. Sales execution is synonymous with qualifying. You are qualifying every step of the way from the first time you speak to a prospect until you get the signature. During this time, you are determining the business value that can be uncovered for the customer. You're positioning your offering against the competition. You're figuring out if this customer will be worth your precious time.

Great sales execution comprises four components: honing your pitch, running quality meetings, negotiating win-win deals, and reliably closing deals. I'll cover the first two in the rest of this chapter and the latter two in the ensuing ones.

HONE YOUR PITCH

Compelling presentations take different forms—slides, videos, demos. What they all have in common is they concisely convey your core insight, establish your credibility, and convincingly lay out your product's value proposition. To understand how to do this effectively, first you need to brainstorm probing discovery questions that will help you connect to the customer.

The right discovery questions unearth customer problems and potential solutions. Brainstorm open-ended questions that establish the customers' priorities and broader context. "What are your top priorities this quarter?" is a standard question, but you can be more probing yet if you've done your homework. For example, "On your last earnings call, I heard your CEO speak about the need to invest more in new product introductions. How is that impacting your group and its priorities?" Keep an updated list of leading questions that effectively uncover pain points and use them in your meetings. The best questions demonstrate an understanding of the customer's business.

I'll never forget one tough meeting. I was the sole representative surrounded by a number of executives from a major player in their industry. After introductions, I started with our usual script asking probing questions about their business. They were polite, but tight-lipped in their responses. Sensing that I wouldn't get far, I fired up our boilerplate sales deck. Their skepticism only deepened. These were grizzled, no-nonsense engineers and here they were listening to me banging my chest about our latest shiny invention.

I wasn't getting anywhere. I had to change tack.

I went for it: "We've heard that forty percent of the productivity on your projects could be unlocked if you just had better tools." It worked. Their body language changed. Their eyes widened; they leaned into their chairs. They started talking about their productivity problems.

I'd found the discovery question that showed some understanding of their business problems. That one nugget, a throwaway comment that their competitor had mentioned to me a few months earlier, established our credibility even though we weren't experts in their space. We signed them to a six-figure deal within six months.

Your pitch should also connect your value proposition to the customer's priorities. Imagine an organization chart with each level and function having a set of priorities. Your job is to understand your buyer persona's priorities, how these fit into the priorities of their division or company, and how your solution could impact these. Back to that tough meeting. I had in fact stumbled upon one of that company's top priorities. I had their attention from then on.

Following is an example of the priorities for a fictitious software company and where you'd fit if you're selling a customer success platform to make their CSMs more productive.

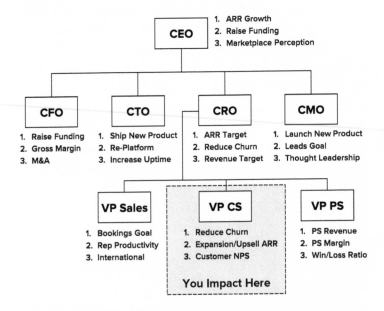

Keep in mind that all the best intel in the world won't do much to move the needle unless you can structure your presentation correctly. Several years ago, Andy Raskin wrote about Zuora's sales deck[52] as the greatest that he'd ever seen. He mentioned five elements that really set the deck apart from the rest. Here's what you need, according to Andy:

1. *Name a big, relevant change in the world.* This should be an "indisputable truth." "E-commerce will accelerate post-COVID19-pandemic" is a good example.

2. *Show there will be winners and losers.* The point here is to give anxiety to the customers that may fall on the losing

---

52 Andy Raskin, "The Greatest Sales Deck I've Ever Seen," Mission,org, September 15, 2016, https://medium.com/the-mission/the-greatest-sales-deck-ive-ever-seen-4f4ef3391ba0.

side. At Videoplaza, we cited the transition from analog to digital in video streaming and monetization with Netflix and Amazon as the winners thus far.

3. *Tease the promised land.* Instead of introducing your product immediately, talk instead about the future state, about your founding insights to give the prospect a glimpse into the future.

4. *Introduce features as magic gifts for overcoming obstacles to the promised land.* This is where your product comes in with its ability to get the customer to the other side.

5. *Present evidence that you can make the story come true.* Case studies, customer testimonials, analyst quotes, product demos—all of these are appropriate in telling this part of the narrative.

I've seen this flow work well, especially for SaaS platforms, and you should give it a try. I've also found that the buildup can be too much, especially when pitching seasoned, highly technical prospects whose skepticism rises the longer you hold information back on your product.

Finally, in your presentation, remember to show, don't tell.

Pictures, and videos, tell a thousand words and then some. Humans respond to visuals, especially of other humans, making for a more emotional connection to your story. Be sure to include powerful visuals or videos in your decks. They'll be more effective than graphs or copy.

But there's no better way of articulating your value proposition than by actually showing it.

It was October 6, 2005, in San Francisco. The prestigious Web

2.0 Conference with speakers such as Mark Cuban, Vinod Khosla, Barry Diller, and Evan Williams, the audience packed with VCs and the digerati. It was going to be Brightcove's coming-out party after operating in stealth mode. How could we make the best impression with the few minutes we'd have on stage? We debated this in the months leading up to the show, considering various scripts and decks. Risky as it might be, we decided to show, not tell.

Brightcove Founder Jeremy Allaire walked onto the stage, said a few words of introduction, and then, in front of everyone's eyes, created and launched a branded streaming video player. Something that would normally take a team weeks, if not months, to create.

It was a smashing success. We were inundated with leads, and not just random ones either. Major publishers like the *New York Times* inquired as did some celebrities. I'll never forget speaking to the legendary Herbie Hancock about creating his own online video channel!

Remember that while you may be solving a business problem, you're pitching to people. They want the story, the visuals, and something to get excited about. Don't inundate them with technical details; simplify your message and make it come to life for them.

Fast-forward to 2006. Jeremy and I found ourselves in the plush NYC office of an executive at Universal Music Group, the walls adorned with framed album covers, pictures with famous artists, a gorgeous Fender guitar on its stand. We huddled in front of a computer screen at his conference table.

UMG executive: "So what brings you here?"

Jeremy Allaire, sweat pouring from his forehead from having run across Manhattan to make it on time: "We're building a video distribution platform to enable publishers to encode, manage, and publish video content over the internet."

UMG executive: "Huh? What does that mean?"

Jeremy: "Our cloud-based platform enables workflows to let content owners easily upload videos, edit metadata, create the user experience and..."

UMG executive: "Huh? What does that even mean?!"

Jeremy, now visibly flustered: "Brightcove empowers content owners to become publishers via their own branded experiences..."

UMG executive erupts: "I have no idea what you're saying. Explain this to me like I'm a six-year-old!"

I cleared my throat. I was sweating too at this point but I had to jump in. My friend Jeff, who'd brokered the meeting, was boring his eyes into me. "We're building a B2B version of You-Tube. Instead of putting your videos up there, you can use our technology to do your own, under your own brand, and keep the revenues."

The penny finally dropped. The executive understood what we did and how it could impact their business. We finished the rest of the meeting and, before long, had won a six-figure contract with UMG. Phew.

Remember, while you live and breathe your technology, your buyer doesn't. You'll have a much better response if you can plainly explain the customer's problem and how you fix it.

RUN QUALITY MEETINGS

Sales meetings take time to set up if you're lucky enough to get one at all. Inefficient meetings lead to longer sales cycles and lost deals. Running better quality meetings is an easy way to move the needle on your sales execution.

A good discovery meeting should indicate whether both parties should continue the dialogue.

Discovery meetings are meant to discover problems and potential solutions for each party to justify spending more time on the relationship. Information should flow both ways. The prospect will feel annoyed if you use up the time asking them questions, especially those that could be answered via some basic research. Conversely, do not "show up and throw up," that is, go through your standard pitch and have the clock run out. You may well annoy the prospect and you won't have learned anything. In an initial meeting, your prospect should have 40 to 60 percent of the airtime.[53]

Last, even if the meeting results in no obvious ways to work together, both parties should feel like they got something out of it.

---

53   Gong.io, a startup that parses sales calls, pegs top reps to talk 46 percent of the time, whereas bottom performers spoke 72 percent of the time. Chris Orlob, "This Is What Separates Your Star Reps From The Rest Of The Team," Gong, November 4, 2017, https://live-gong-2020.pantheonsite.io/blog/this-is-what-separates-your-star-reps-from-the-rest-of-the-team.

Do your homework.

Annual reports. Press releases. Websites. There is so much information at our fingertips, making it so easy to prepare before a big meeting. And yet, you'd be surprised at how often people show up at a meeting and wing it. Even worse, they ask basic, even stupid, questions that a cursory search could have answered. This really annoys me when I'm on the buy side. It indicates a lack of respect for my time. Don't be that rep.

Use creative icebreakers.

Engineers often think you can plow forward in a sales meeting, but that's not how it really works. Meetings just feel too weird without icebreakers. For millennia, humans have used some common context, some sort of icebreaker to try to establish trust when meeting strangers. Back in the day, it would be weather or trading route gossip. Today it's sports, weather, or traffic.

Be different. Maybe you noticed some artwork in their office that you appreciate. In meetings where you've had an introduction from someone, that common person is a great way to establish a connection. Whatever you do, don't bring up that picture of your prospect on her wedding day as part of the googling you did pre-meeting. That's just creepy.

The customer should go first to set the context.

The flow of a typical thirty-minute discovery meeting should be introductions followed by you asking them your discovery questions followed by your company introduction. You want to establish why they are taking the meeting in the first place, their priorities and perspective. That sets the stage for you to talk about your differentiated value proposition.

Actively listen. Drill down into their problems. Keep probing.

Bad sales meetings happen when the rep talks past the customer, waiting for them to finish speaking to launch into their script. The best sales reps listen like detectives, ferreting out clues and connecting the dots. For example, if the prospect says, "Increasing the uptime of our robot is one of our biggest challenges," it ought to lead to several more lines of questioning from you: What's the current uptime and what should it be? What are the most common failure modes that lead to downtime? What have they tried already and what solutions do they think hold the most promise? What would it mean if the status quo were to continue?

Respectfully challenge the prospect if they are not sharing enough.

Sometimes the prospect just doesn't give up information. They're at a secretive company or theirs is a "need to know" project that you don't need to know. These prospects want to hear pitches and decide for themselves.

If this is the case, you have the right to challenge them for more information. After all, it's your precious time as well. You could say something like, "Can we level set here…we're happy to share about what we're doing but we find that our best engagements are where there is close collaboration with our customers as our product isn't out of the box. We also have limited resources as to which engagements we take on. I respect your desire for secrecy, but we don't have much to go on and it'll be hard for us to justify engaging further if we don't get a better sense of whether there could be a fit."

They'll respond in either of two ways:

1. You'll jolt them into sharing more information and you can continue the dialogue.
2. They'll hold firm and you'll need to make a decision. This depends on the context. I'll often qualify out especially as this can indicate a lack of cultural fit with the customer. But there are certain instances, typically in monopsony contexts where there's only one or a few buyers, where you may have to hold your nose and do their bidding. For instance, if you're selling chips to smartphone makers, you won't have a choice if Apple insists on just hearing you out.

Don't be afraid to (politely) qualify out.

Often, it will be clear early on that there really isn't a fit. Gracefully exit the conversation while leaving the door open: "Thanks so much for that background. To be honest, unless I missed something, I don't really see a fit here. I don't want to waste your time any further. We appreciate your time and let's keep in touch in case things change."

You'll be surprised at how sometimes people will qualify you back in, immediately sharing more information or brainstorming how your solution could be a fit.

Keep the meeting interactive. Nodding heads do not signal agreement or understanding.

Optimize for engagement. That's how you'll learn the most about the customer and the potential fit. It's also how you'll engender trust. Draw the customer into the conversation.

A common mistake is to interpret a lack of questions or even head nods of murmured assent as understanding. People don't want to look bad in front of others. They will nod their heads to be polite, especially when there is a language barrier. Ask for feedback as you pitch. Ask more pointed questions if you're not getting much engagement: "Kim, not to put you on the spot, but I'm curious as to your take on what we just discussed, especially as I know you've spent a long time working on these problems."

Keep to the agenda. Park discussions that are tangents and risk derailing the meeting.

Remember, the goal of the meeting is to discover whether your value proposition is a potential fit for the customer and how it could impact their top priorities. Often, you'll get asked about something tangential by someone wanting to sound smart. Hold the line at being drawn into the rabbit hole without being rude: "Great question, I'll say a few words now but that can be another meeting on its own. I suggest we park that and come back to it. There's a lot more to discuss from the agenda we agreed on. Thank you for raising this topic, though; let's follow up offline to discuss."

The exception is if the decision-maker commandeers the meeting and takes it off agenda. You can try bringing it back to the agenda, but it will be awkward and could alienate your counterpart. In these cases, I'd call out the diversion and have an ask: "Lee, it's intriguing that you think our solution could impact your goal on retention. To be candid, we'd focused our preparation on how we could impact your team's productivity. It sounds like retention is more important to you at this point and so we're happy to wing it, but we were also excited about how we could impact productivity. Could we schedule a follow-up on that at some point?"

Use an upcoming meeting to get more information and to better position yourself.

You have a big pitch meeting upcoming with the right stakeholders. Agree on the agenda with the person setting up the meeting beforehand. Get on a call with them to do this and use that time to probe further and ensure the best use of time. Knowing the attendees, their priorities, and any sensitivities will be invaluable to your preparation. For instance, you'll want to know if someone attending built the homegrown solution that you'd be getting rid of. Your counterpart will be motivated to ensure a productive meeting or else it will reflect poorly on them.

You have more power than you think. Use it. Ensure that the "gives and gets" are proportional.

First-time founders mistakenly ascribe too much power to their prospects. This manifests in sharing too much information, demos, and access to yourself without getting enough in return. Don't make this mistake.

Remember, the customer has big problems that you, with your insight, team, and technology, are uniquely suited to solve. The companies you're selling to are worried about being disrupted from below or having their direct competitors steal a march on them. They need innovation, which you represent, to surpass the competition and prevent disruption.

There should be a healthy reciprocal dynamic as you engage prospects. For instance, what would you want from a customer "in exchange" for getting a demo? Most of the time, this will be implicit, but there are times when you'll need to call this out and ensure a fair transaction: "We are happy to give you a demo. Before I prioritize this for my engineering team, we'd need to better understand your use cases so we can make sure it's as relevant for you as possible."

Explicitly ask for feedback. Have the customer play the value back to you.

Receiving candid feedback is paramount when pitching. You won't know what went right, or more importantly, wrong, unless you hear directly from the customer. One effective tactic, toward the end of the meeting, is to ask the customer for their impressions. I like to say, "In the final minutes, I'd love to zoom out a level and get your take on what you've seen or heard and how it matches your expectations." If they answer with polite platitudes, probe further: "Are there specific areas that resonated for you and also ones that you have concern about that we ought to know?"

A related tactic is asking them to play your value back to you.[54] This works especially well when the customer has been reticent to give feedback. I was nervous to do this when this was first taught to me. What if the customer couldn't do so? What if I didn't like what I heard? But that's the point. You want to know if you landed your value proposition or what parts of the pitch didn't stick, something like, "You've clearly seen a lot and are very advanced in your thinking. I'm curious, what value do you see, if any, in what we're doing?"

Seek informal interactions during your visit. These are often where you'll get the most valuable information.

---

54 This is also effective when negotiating. If the customer is beating you down on terms, have them play the value back to you to know what they actually value and what they don't.

At Brightcove, I often had the humbling experience of being the lone reason that the meeting was being held in English rather than the native language of the people in the room. Speakers of a second language subconsciously act more reserved, so we wouldn't get a lot of candid feedback. One effective tactic would be for me to find a reason to leave our rep alone with the prospect before leaving their office. Those few minutes would give our local sales rep the chance to probe his counterparts for feedback in their native language.

I remember one pitch we'd given at Videoplaza to a French broadcaster. It was a highly structured affair with poker faces throughout. We only learned where we stood versus the competition after the meeting when I'd excused myself for a quick break. Those few moments made the whole meeting worthwhile.

Build these informal interactions into your pitching. If someone on the customer's team offers you coffee, take them up on it and have someone on your team accompany them to the kitchen. Make those few minutes count and don't just talk about the weather or sports; try to get some pointed questions in as they'll have their guard down. While it's tougher to do this when pitching remotely, try private messaging or, for certain customers, inviting them to a common Slack channel.

Bonus points for impromptu meetings with others during a meeting.

Sometimes, your contact will introduce you to other stakeholders outside of the meeting. This is a great sign. Perhaps it's their boss who was double-booked. They don't have time to properly meet you, but your contact thinks she can step out of her call for a quick hello and handshake. Take the offer! Be prepared to give your elevator pitch and, more importantly, an ask along the lines of "Sue, we've been getting more and more excited about the possibility of working together. Your team has been a pleasure to deal with and we'll continue to do that, but it would be great to be able to give you updates from time to time." You now have permission to access (and escalate to) the executive.

Meeting other stakeholders who represent "power" is key, even if they weren't originally invited. Back-office functions like legal, finance, procurement, and IT are often not invited to pitch meetings. And yet they are key in facilitating the deal or gumming up the works. At Brightcove, we were pitching the record labels on distributing their videos directly on the internet—an alien concept at the time. While their BD executives were our champions, we knew we'd have to educate legal and accounting in particular and get them on board. We tried to meet these people during a visit even if they weren't invited to the meeting itself. Putting a face to a name and looking someone in the eye is a better way to forge a connection than an impersonal email. Use face-to-face meetings as opportunities to expand your network within the account.

Change the playing field so it's on your turf.

The incumbent's "field" is having a feature-rich product or being a safe pair of hands. You'll need to redefine the frame of reference to favor your value proposition while aligning with the customer's priorities. Oftentimes it means aligning on innovation or speed in contrast to the incumbent.

Avoid free consultancy.

Some prospects will ask a lot of you. They'll want proposals, white papers, demos, and workshops, with nothing concrete coming out of it. Intentionally or not, they are using you for free consultancy. Don't be afraid to escalate this, letting them know that, while you'd be thrilled to work with them as a customer, you are a startup with limited resources and will have no choice but to focus your team elsewhere if they don't move forward.

Always be closing.

Every quality meeting should end with a call to action and a mini-close. Make this a habit of every customer interaction and it will help you when it's time to get a signature. Follow up with what both parties agreed would be the next step in the process. That makes a good reference for the next meeting and holds everyone accountable.

Use workshops to break through interminable discovery processes.

Here's a situation you may have faced: You've been engaged with a prospect for a while. Both parties like each other and talk about working together but nothing ever sticks, no momentum ever gets created, no project seems important enough to get attention from them. There's definitely not a qualified deal for your pipeline and yet you think there's something there, so you don't want to qualify out. How do you handle this?

Propose a workshop. Maybe it's on-site or remote. Whatever the format, it should involve both parties investing time into preparation and the workshop itself. Agree to the agenda beforehand and optimize for interactivity. Each party should present to the other with the bulk of time for Q and A and brainstorming. Stack rank the potential projects by value to the customer and best fit for your product. If there isn't a clear project or two coming out of this, best to qualify out and agree to stay in touch. Even if this is the case, both parties should feel like it was worth the effort.

A QUICK WORD ON RFPS

The golden rule with RFPs is to not bother filling one out if you haven't been involved in writing it. Vendors get a steal on their competition by influencing the writing of an RFP to favor their proposition.

Refuse to respond to unsolicited RFPs unless you can speak to the stakeholders.

Big company procurement organizations have rules on the minimum number of submissions to ensure healthy competition in bids. You're probably receiving an unsolicited RFP (influenced by your competition) to hit procurement's minimum submission target. In these situations, insist on speaking to the authors and challenge them as to why they want to hear from you and what they see in the competition. At the very least, you'll gain insight. Best case, you've turned the tables and are in a power position where they very much want you to bid and so they qualify you in.

Challenging the RFP is a high-risk tactic to tilt the field in your favor.

Use this tactic if the RFP is stacked against you and yet the customer is missing the bigger picture. "We respectfully believe you aren't asking the right questions in this RFP." Then go on to define the questions they should care about and why. Best case is that you win the respect of the customers and get them to pause the RFP and reframe it based on this new understanding. The risk is that you alienate the authors, making them look bad in front of their management.

The one reason to respond to unsolicited RFPs is to get on the company's radar.

Weigh the benefit of getting on the radar against the cost of responding and all the information you'll be sharing. The costs tend to outweigh the benefits, but make your own calculation and decide.

We've covered a lot in this chapter, but that's because the sales pitch and process, including how you get the most out of your interactions, is vital to achieving sales velocity and repeatable sales. Take some time with this information and audit your existing processes as precisely as possible. Nailing these will pay off with smoother processes and more deals closed.

When you're ready, tackle the next step to great sales execution: consistently negotiating win-win deals.

CHAPTER 10

NEGOTIATE WIN-WIN DEALS

It's March 2014. I'm standing on the rim of the Snæfellsjökull glacier in Iceland. I'd whisked my girlfriend at the time[55] on a holiday weekend to spot the northern lights.[56] My phone starts buzzing. It's Sorosh, Videoplaza's CEO. He knows I'm away so he wouldn't disturb me unless it was important. I pick up. Bad news.

There goes the rest of my relaxing getaway.

For much of 2013, we'd been negotiating a strategic partnership with MTG, one of Europe's largest broadcasting groups. Their new chief digital officer, formerly at Google, had hit it off with Sorosh and been architecting a deal whereby MTG would lead a new financing round while becoming our largest customer. Beyond the millions in revenues, Videoplaza would strategically

---

55   She's now my wife!

56   Alas, the northern lights were elusive that weekend so they remain on the bucket list! At least it didn't affect my relationship—we wed a year later and have been happily married since.

benefit by having MTG inventory flow through our platform and not our competition.

Everything had been negotiated and we were deep in diligence. The deal should have closed by year-end, but it didn't happen. My antennae were up. I'm paranoid when deals drag on. But they made the right noises, even talking about what the press release should have in it when we announced the relationship.

Alas, my fears were well-founded. Sorosh was calling to inform me that they'd decided not to invest. Even worse, their operational team, without the top-down mandate to use us, would not move forward as a customer and, even worse, was evaluating our competitor. Fuck.

We scrambled. We tried every angle. We offered to renegotiate terms, added board member pressure, guilt—all to no avail. We lost both the investment and commercial deals.

For now, let's assume you've run the process, qualified the fit, and shaped a solution that will solve a business problem for the customer. They've asked you for a proposal and you're getting into negotiations. How do you get from here to a signature? First, determine how best to structure the deal. I'll then cover techniques to navigate complex deals.

STRUCTURE WIN-WIN DEALS

Before you can present a win-win deal, you must understand it. Sketch out the fundamental value exchange for each party. The customer is hiring you to solve certain problems and achieve value. That is the foundation of your working together. Like any foundation, it needs to be strong and will be tested over time.

Sometimes, when you're seemingly down a dead end, reverting to the first principles will illuminate another way forward.

If you're negotiating an OEM deal with a customer that will embed your sensor into their IoT solution, the fundamentals of the deal might be:

	You	Customer
Motivations	Revenue	Differentiate their product
	Customer reference	Future-proof their business
Must-haves	Minimum order quantities	Fair price/ROI
	Case study	Guaranteed supply
		Integration support
Nice-to-haves	Upfront payment	Exclusivity

Understand the gives and gets from both parties' perspectives. These should be proportional to the value being created (and not just the value of the deal itself). **The contours of any deal are generally around scope or value, cost or risk, and time. You and the customer will negotiate within this framework.**

For instance, if the customer wants you to drop everything to work on their application so they can make a market window, price in the risk you'd be taking by deferring other activities in favor of them. On the other hand, if they ask for a feature that falls next on your road map, you need not price that at a premium.

Decide what's most important to you and what you're willing to give on, then find a way to propose a construct that lets the customer achieve their most important objectives. I just helped a startup negotiate one of their first enterprise contracts. There were two tiers of pricing, but the customer had a time-to-market objective for Tier 1, whereas they couldn't properly scope and thus value Tier 2. At the same time, getting their logo and payment upfront was most important to us. So, we agreed to kick the Tier 2 can down the road in exchange for being paid upfront annually and being able to use their logo. Win-win.

Optimize the following terms.

While there's too much variability to get into the weeds of structuring deals, the following terms are most important for startups of your stage:

- **Term/Renewal/Termination:** Bias toward a longer term. Termination window should reflect the product integration. The lighter the lift, the shorter the termination window.
- **Commitment:** Minimum commits are important and a term I fight hard for. They reflect customer engagement and provide more certainty for business planning.
- **Marketing:** You want referenceable customers and should be willing to give on other terms to be able to do a case study, PR, and other marketing activities. For products involving hardware installations, having a customer willing to host prospective customers to see your product in action is gold, much more powerful than an office visit.
- **Payment Terms:** Net 30–net 90 payment terms are most common. Larger, more complex deals, especially selling to government entities, may be even greater than that. Getting paid upfront is great to optimize cash runway, so be willing to trade off other terms for this.
- **Preference:** Early adopter customers often ask for exclusivity to give them a competitive advantage and in recognition

for the risk they're taking in working with you. **Do NOT give exclusivity away lightly.** It can come back to bite you in future financings, M&A, or deals, even if it seems like a small give at the time. You can compromise along the following non-mutually exclusive dimensions:

- *Scope/Application Exclusivity*: Define as narrow a scope as possible for the customer to have preference.
- *Geo Restriction*: Define a territory preference.
- *Time to Market*: You agree to not offer your product or certain features to the market for a period of time after providing to the customer.
- *Carve-out*: The customer names X competitors that you agree not to work with for a defined period of time.
- *First Look*: The customer is front of the line for any new features you roll out so they can steal a march on their competition.
- *Right of First Refusal (ROFR)*: Before accepting any competing offer, you must first allow your customer to match or beat it. This is a rare clause in commercial agreements.
- *Most Favored Nations (MFN)*: You agree that the customer will get the same or better pricing terms as similarly situated customers. This protects the early customer from having others get better commercial terms despite the risk they've taken.

- **Road Map Influence:** Early customers demand this for good reason, fearing that their needs will be subsumed by others. There are several ways to give them comfort in this regard:
  - *Quarterly Briefings / Customer Advisory Board*: This is a classic tool used by both Sales and Product Management to assure a customer that their voice will be heard. The notion of being able to influence road map is also appealing to early adopters.
  - *Dedicated or Ring-fenced Professional Services*: Carving

out PS resources, ideally funded by the customer, dedicated to the customer's projects with you can also solve the customer's need for control while giving you the freedom to execute on your broader road map. This should be done sparingly, assuming your APIs and integration points are up to snuff, and only for the largest, most strategic accounts.

○ *Road Map Commitments*: Sometimes you just need to commit to certain features in order to win a deal. Again, be reticent to offer these up or risk having your team tied up with commitments and unable to respond to market changes.

Think like an investor on shared risk, shared upside deals.

Most garden-variety deals involve a standard customer–vendor dynamic. The former pays the latter for their product. There may be deals involving shared risk and upside, revenue sharing being the most common. These can be lucrative, but you'll want to evaluate them like an investor, including doing due diligence, creating a business case, scenario planning risks and upsides, and taking a portfolio approach by assuming some percent of them won't work out as envisioned.

Minimize the number of signatures.

It's hard to get signatures. Enterprises require vendors to jump through various hoops for good reason—to reduce risk. The fewer signatures it takes to work with you, the more inertia you have baked in to continue to work with the customer. Here are a few tactics to consider to reduce friction.

• **Automated Renewals:** I have a strong bias for automated renewal in contracts. Both parties can leave but there is positive momentum built in. It also prevents liability risk where both parties forgot to renew and are technically out of contract, which happens more than you'd think!

- **Master Service Agreements (MSAs):** These put a framework in place with terms and conditions that govern working together with addenda or POs that can be placed without having to negotiate the entire framework.
- **POs/Online Ts & Cs:** Consult your lawyer as to whether you can use online terms and conditions with a simple PO as your standard form.

DEAL NAVIGATION TECHNIQUES

Complex deals are challenging even for seasoned sales executives, let alone technical founders. It's hard to understand where you stand, and the path to a win is foggy. Use the following principles to navigate such situations.

Hierarchically engage customers.

Match the customer's hierarchy with your own. If they have an executive sponsor, the project owner, and an engineering team, limit your engagement to the executive sponsor, your sales rep to the project owner, and your FAE to the engineering team. You can then be an escalation point with your executive counterpart. You want the customer to see you as being above the fray (even though you will very much be in the weeds!) and the person to whom your rep will escalate customer negotiation requests for approval.

If you are the primary rep, it's hard to cultivate a lateral relationship with both your counterpart and the executive sponsor, and awkward to say no to requests. In these cases, bring in a rep so you can focus upward, bring in a board member to be the executive counterpart, and use your board to escalate requests.

Keep close to the customer.

Conducting a regular dialogue with the customer across communication channels is a great way of building a relationship and maintaining momentum. Try scheduling a weekly check-in call and use text or Slack for more informal interactions. This will help you keep a pulse on how things are progressing. Regular communication is also the first thing to go if your customer has chosen your competitor. That said, there is a fine line between being perseverant and creepy. Know where this is and don't cross it.

Map the power at your customer.

Back to the MTG deal. How did we lose it? It came down to power, a concept in Value Selling that is easily applicable outside of it.[57] Power is anyone that can veto the deal. It can reside with your main interlocutor and be both hierarchical and lateral. Power is most obvious in the form of the C-suite or the board; however, it can also reside below. Executives tend to want the support of their tech teams to move forward on a new platform, fearing a lack of adoption if there isn't buy-in. Lateral examples of power include IT, procurement, and legal, each of which have their own agendas.

In enterprise accounts, first map the terrain. Try and get an understanding of the power and their priorities. How have they

---

57   Value Selling is a framework I've used at Ooyala and brought to others.

viewed propositions or companies similar to yours? Where does your project fit within their priorities? Who haven't you met that you need to get in front of to get the deal over the line? Getting in front of these people with your story is best. It's a lot harder to nix something after you've invested time with someone. You may not be able to meet with all of the power, but knowing where it resides is also useful as it will indicate where the risks are and enable you to better forecast your pipeline. As Carlos Nouche, of ValueSelling Associates, likes to say, "You can still get deals done without having covered the power. That's called getting lucky."

We'd put too much faith in our champion, the CDO, our main conduit at MTG. Turns out, he hadn't properly gotten their CFO on board. The CFO, doing his job, challenged the deal, asking why MTG was doing a minority investment in a tech company when it typically does majority investments in content companies. Great question and one that the CDO wasn't prepared to answer. Being new to his role, he realized he didn't have the credibility to get it through and wasn't going to spend his political capital on us, so the deal died.

Negotiate based on principles.

The best negotiators articulate principles so as not to appear arbitrary and refer to these over time.[58] Establish and constantly refer to principles that align with the motivations for each party. Using the example from the start of this chapter:

- **Your mission.** Referring to your North Star when negotiating terms helps navigate tricky situations since your mission is nonnegotiable. "I understand why you'd want exclusivity

---

58   I learned this from the classic book on negotiating, *Getting to Yes*, well worth a read.

but having our product only available through one channel just wouldn't align with our mission to be the most widely distributed location sensor for robots."

- **Running a long-term sustainable business.** "We'd love to give you a lower price, but it won't be sustainable. It will benefit you in the long run to ensure a key supplier of yours with a healthy business."
- **Fairness.** "I'm afraid we just can't get to that pricing. It wouldn't be fair to our earlier customers who took larger risks early on and have been able to justify our pricing."
- **Opportunity cost.** Often missed in negotiations, your opportunity cost of spinning up your team to integrate and support a customer is far greater than the dollars they may pay. You'll be rejecting or sequencing other opportunities by taking the customer on, so the overall deal potential has to reflect these opportunity costs.

Dig into the "why" behind their asks.

Don't take your counterpart's requests at face value. Probe deeper to the underlying motivations. Why do they want a lower price? To look good in front of their bosses? To have budget left over in case the project goes sideways? To fill gaps in your product? I could go on. You can then address the real reason behind their ask.

For example, you divine that the customer really wants to reduce their risk on an unproven technology. You can then lower their risk in other ways, whether by making pricing contingent on certain milestones, giving them a service-level agreement (SLA) with more teeth, or even giving them a grace period to be able to get out of the deal. If they are asking for something that isn't standard, understanding the why behind their request will always help you give something you're comfortable with that they will find valuable as well.

Negotiate holistically "as a package." Don't let the customer divide and conquer.

Construct and negotiate your proposals holistically. Maybe you've given a lower price in recognition of the customer's willingness to do a case study. Or you're willing to waive setup fees if they can move fast on the deal. These terms are linked and should be communicated as such.

Enterprises, intentionally or not, often negotiate in piecemeal. You'll send them your agreement and then get one set of comments from the business owner, another round of edits from legal, and yet another round from procurement, making concessions each round. If this is the case, state that you will negotiate holistically and ask them to make their requests as a package. Otherwise, you risk a bad deal by a thousand cuts.

Always be de-risking.

I encounter this one often. I hear, "We went far down the path with XYZ but they ended up choosing another option." Either that or they stay with the status quo. In these cases, it usually comes down to too much risk for the customer. Risk that they're betting on an unproven tech or young company versus continuing with the status quo or a safe pair of hands. Brainstorm how you can de-risk their decision. Try termination rights, road map sessions, SLAs, software in escrow, right to manufacture, and warranties as tools to reduce the customer's risk.

Sometimes you just need to buy a deal.

You are trying to penetrate a new market and desperately need a reference customer. Acme Corporation, with its reputation as a first mover, would be the best such reference. Where Acme goes, the rest follow. The problem is that Acme already works with your direct competitor, effectively freezing you out of the account and the broader vertical.

Then, in one of your periodic check-ins, your contact at Acme indicates all is not well with your competitor's installation, that they're going out to bid. The door into Acme, and their vertical, has just cracked open. **You need to buy the deal.**

Buying a deal means making an offer that's too good to pass up. It could be price, preference, services, business model, or other entitlements like offering them warrants in your business. Buying deals is risky business. Word can get out and others may want the same type of deal. Or the deal can be more expensive for you than you'd thought.

Buy a deal only if it's really strategic: to enter a new market, get referenceable customers, or prevent competition from entering. Treat it as a marketing expense and make sure you get expected value as you would with any significant marketing investment.

Buy deals if there are sequencing dynamics in the industry.

Some industries display a herd mentality in that the herd will follow whatever the early adopter leaders do. In these cases, negotiate aggressively to land the early adopter, buying the deal if you need to.

Sequencing is very much present in the UK TV broadcast market. Sky TV, the pay TV operator, has a history of adopting innovation in technologies relative to Channel 4, ITV, and smaller broadcasters. Sky prides themselves on being at the forefront of innovation. Nailing Sky was key to the rest of the UK.

And so, it played out that way for us at Brightcove. My former boss, Elisabeth Bentel Carpenter, used to work at Sky and booked what we thought was an informational meeting. We had no UK presence at the time. They moved quickly and we'd signed them to a contract within weeks of our first meeting. There's nothing like the start of the Premier League season to focus minds! We nailed Sky and, within the next year, landed deals with Channel 4, ITV, and BBC Worldwide.

Fast-forward a few years. Sky was looking to better monetize their digital video ad inventory and conducted a bakeoff between Videoplaza (the company I would end up joining) and FreeWheel, the US competitor. They narrowly chose FreeWheel despite Videoplaza's local presence. It effectively shut Videoplaza out of the UK market. Despite years of trying and having our HQ in London, we were only able to land a couple of small UK accounts amounting to less than $100,000 per year in revenues combined. That's the power of sequencing and the importance of landing the early adopter in such markets.

Leave something on the table for procurement and/or executives.

If you know that procurement will get involved in a deal, hold something back so you can "give" on these when they do get involved. That will make them feel like they're doing a good job. This can also apply to the executive who will sign off on the deal. I was once counseled by my counterpart that his boss always asked for an extra 5 percent discount off the price before signing an agreement. Hint taken.

Identify the signer and understand their process.

As you get into a deal, you should understand who will sign and their process to get a signature. If you don't know this for the later-stage deals in your pipeline, move them back a stage until you do.

Leave outs to let your counterpart save face.

Negotiations can get heated. When they do, always be sure to leave face-saving ways out for yourself and your counterpart. People hate being backed into a corner and hate capitulating. A graceful way out may be to make a concession that doesn't really matter to you but has optics that will help your counterpart save face.

Project confidence.

Technical founders tend to unnecessarily give concessions. This stems from a lack of confidence in themselves or their value proposition. An advisee founder recently negotiated a large deal for their company and gave away dozens of professional services hours as well as a discount on the license.[59] They didn't need to do so. The customer clearly wanted their product. So have confidence in what you have and resist the urge to, in enterprise sales parlance, "drop your pants."

Be not afraid of hearing no. It will help you get to yes.

When I started out in sales, I was afraid to hear "no" from the customer. I'd do whatever it'd take to not hear "no," making

---

59   Thankfully, we were able to walk some of the concessions back and got to a win-win deal involving a minimum of $200,000 a year over three years…pretty meaningful for a ten-person startup!

promises, avoiding subjects, hearing what I wanted to hear. With experience, I now know that customer nos are rich signals that should be mined. Complex negotiations often butt up against one party's refusal to budge on a particular point. Most large transactions like M&A deals involve situations where each party is testing the other's limits and where nos are inevitable on the path to getting a deal done. Don't be afraid to ask hard questions that may yield a no. Better to know that upfront. The worst outcome in sales is getting to a slow no.

Be not afraid of saying no.

Having the confidence to say no was a force multiplier in my sales career. Customers respect well-reasoned nos from vendors. They've too often been disappointed by yes-reps, whose products can magically do everything. Saying no, especially the ultimate no of walking from a deal, forces the customer's hand. They will often qualify you back in. And if they don't, well, you've learned that they don't see enough value, that they don't care.

I've covered how to run quality sales meetings and negotiate deals on the path to great sales execution. Next up, the hardest aspect of sales: closing.

CHAPTER 11

RELIABLY CLOSE DEALS

Cologne, Germany. Winter of 2012.

I was visiting RTL Deutschland, one of Europe's largest broadcasters and by far the biggest deal in Videoplaza's pipeline. We were a year into our process with them. We knew they were serious about using us but had been having a hard time getting them to commit both financially and to moving forward. Germans are notoriously slow-moving when it comes to business.[60] And yet, the deal was make-or-break for us. The revenue was baked into our Series B story and 2013 budget.

The meeting was to introduce me, the newest executive, to the broadcaster's leadership, and to progress the deal. We'd gone through our presentation and the points on the deal itself, addressing their concerns as they were raised. There was some murmuring and head-nodding but they wouldn't be drawn on committing. All the while, the clock was ticking before we'd have to leave for the airport to catch our flights.

---

60   They are heavily consensus-driven and notoriously conservative. However, once they commit, they're in it for the long haul.

So, I went for the close.

"Gentlemen, I understand we've been discussing this partnership for quite some time, well before I joined Videoplaza. We certainly believe in the overall opportunity to work together to increase your video revenues and future-proof you against Google and others. At the same time, our opportunity costs continue to grow. We will need you to commit to be able to justify continued resources and to hit the aggressive integration timelines that our teams have sketched. Is that something you're prepared to do?"

I lived many lifetimes in those next few moments. Our rep's eyes grew big. Big-shot execs are not to be put on the spot.

It worked. After some posturing, they agreed to move forward at a seven-figure minimum commit. We didn't have the signature, but their assent was enough. We signed the formal agreement within a couple of months, and we were on our way to exceeding our 2013 number.

Closing is the hardest part of sales. In most enterprise deals, there's that uncomfortable moment of truth where you ask the customer to commit. This may not feel natural, but you need to develop this muscle and hire reps who can close. Time and time again, I've seen reps who can prospect, give good presentations, and build what seems to be a solid pipeline, but not seal the deal. Their deals, constantly on the cusp of signing, keep slipping to the next quarter.

Use these closing techniques at appropriate times during your process:

- **The soft close.** A soft close is conditional and gives both you and the prospect a way out in case they don't go for it. "If we're able to sign up to the SLA your IT team has requested, would you be comfortable in moving forward with the rest of the deal?"
- **The assumptive close.** This is where you assume positive intent and momentum. "Given your feedback on our proposal, I think we're close and so I've taken the liberty of having our lawyer draw up a draft agreement and will have them send it to you by the end of the week." You don't want to appear heavy-handed, but customers also appreciate thoughtful, prescriptive gestures from their vendors.
- **The hard close.** The most fraught type, involving a "take it or leave it" ultimatum. Use sparingly as it can risk alienation or worse. And be prepared to follow through or you'll lose credibility.

Always be closing—redux.

As discussed in Chapter 8, every customer interaction should have some sort of mini close to keep the process going. These mini transactions, like signing a nondisclosure agreement or booking a workshop, will get you used to closing so that the final ask to sign the agreement won't seem as awkward.

Be not afraid of awkward silence.

Inexperienced reps speak too much. They try to fill in the silences after having stated their position. Avoid this temptation. If you present your position, let the customer react or speak, even if it means an awkward silence. I've had negotiations where I was literally waiting for fifteen to twenty seconds after speaking for their reaction.

Do not negotiate against yourself.

The worst is to backtrack without hearing the customer's response. This is called negotiating against yourself. It signals a lack of confidence and that there is more room to give. In any negotiation, let the other party give you their perspective before conceding anything.

Put a mutual plan in place to get to signature and beyond.

Another powerful concept from Value Selling is the mutual plan. This is a written framework between you and the customer as to the steps each party will take to realizing value. It's a great tool to hold each other accountable and serves as a turn-by-turn guide to navigating the deal. This is a living document and should be updated and referred to at every interaction. The hardest part is making this mutual. You may have the ideal plan, but the customer needs to buy into this as well.

Be sensitive to momentum. Time kills deals.

Momentum. You'll know it when you have it. You have a regular cadence with the customer. Each party follows up promptly on action items. Emails and calls are returned on a timely basis. You also know it when you've lost it. Action items drag on, unfinished. Calls don't get returned or worse yet (and a pet peeve of mine), they go radio silent and ghost you altogether.

Deals are won and lost on momentum. Once-hot deals drag on and then the world changes. One of my companies had signed a term sheet in early 2020 for a funding round but the diligence kept dragging. Then the COVID-19 pandemic hit and the lead VC backed out, leaving them to scramble to put a bridge round together.

Do what you can to increase momentum and don't be afraid to be aggressive and creative: Does your counterpart have a hard time getting their legal to review your agreement? Offer to have your lawyer fly to their office to hash out the deal. Keep the momentum going.

Use forcing functions to unstick stalled deals.

The bane of my existence, stalled deals drive us all crazy. Stalled deals almost always reflect changing customer priorities, i.e., your project is no longer in their top three objectives. Forcing functions can unstick stalled deals. Use them sparingly and don't bluff so that you can maintain credibility.

- **The Upcoming Board Meeting:** "Can we get this deal done in time for our board meeting next month? This deal is strategic and will require their approval and we would hate to have to wait until the next one." I've at times invited my counterpart at the customer to speak at a board meeting. That kind of exposure can be very motivating to certain people *and* it's also useful to the board to hear directly from a customer in an intimate setting. Win-win.
- **Competing for Scarce Resources:** Another way to goad slower-moving processes into action is to convey competition for your scarce resources. "We've been in discussions for a while. We would be thrilled to work together but, candidly, we have other customers whose projects would involve the same resources we would use for your project. Since we're a startup with limited resources, we'll need to allocate my team to other projects unless we can reach an agreement by the end of this month." Or else something like, "We're producing a limited run of units for our lighthouse customer program. The other units are spoken for and so you have an

opportunity to fill this last spot. If we can't agree on terms by the end of the month, we'll need to offer your unit to someone else on the wait list." You'll know how important your project is based on their reaction.

- **The External Event:** "We're planning a big launch event next spring and will be showcasing our work with key lighthouse customers. We anticipate getting lots of press attention given the nature of our product. We'd love for you to be one of them, but we'll need to get this deal done by X date to have enough time." This is obviously particularly useful with companies and people that value PR and being seen as early adopters.

Presenting forcing functions may still get you a "Thanks for letting us know but we still won't be able to move forward for now" kind of response. That's fine; at least you know where you really stand and will be able to forecast the deal more accurately.

Close down optionality and park open items to keep deal momentum.

Let's say you're negotiating an agreement for a division of a large company to use your platform. At some point, they ask for pricing and other terms to enable other divisions to come on board. This is great but can also delay if not sidetrack the deal. Keep the deal moving. Add a term if it's easy to do and amenable to them, such as the right for other divisions at the company to leverage the same terms as this one. But don't if it means further negotiation or due diligence.

Instead, suggest that you focus on closing this first agreement to be able to start the division's onboarding and come back to a broader construct later. Adding some contract language like

"The terms of this license may be superseded by future agreements" can assuage concerns. It states the obvious but can be a comfort to customers, nonetheless.

Don't sell past the close.

The customer agrees to your terms. You're moving to a formal agreement. Now is not the time to bring up that new road map feature you're building or that you're standing up a customer support organization. This is called selling past the close. The customer already wants to work with you. By selling past the close, you may be confusing them or worse, introducing a reason to stall the deal so they can further evaluate.

Be paranoid and persistent—a deal isn't done until you have the signature.

I'll never forget my first call with Pablo Silva when I was at Brightcove. He was a digital executive at Fox UK. We'd been trying to get into that account for a while with no luck. I finally got him on the phone. "It's great to speak to you but, to be honest, it's probably too late. I literally have a contract with Ooyala (Brightcove's direct competitor) sitting on my desk waiting for my signature." We quickly ran through some points of differentiation and asked him to give us some time to put a deal together that he couldn't refuse. "I'll give you until next Monday to convince me that you're a better partner." It was Thursday.

We got on it. Our CEO wrote him a comprehensive email as to how we were a better long-term fit. We simultaneously worked with our CFO to put a very attractive deal together. We wanted to get into Fox. We hustled and won the deal from under the nose of our competitor, Ooyala,[61] whose rep had probably marked that deal as in the bag. It was one of the most satisfying deals in my career. Hustle and perseverance go a long way. By that same token, a deal isn't closed until you get the signature. Be paranoid, be persistent.

HANDLING LOST DEALS

It sucks to lose deals. How you and your team handle these will be important and sets the tone for your sales culture. When it happens, don't panic. First, evaluate if it's actually really lost. Customers are constantly hearing new pitches and can start leaning in another direction. Going cold can be a negotiating tactic. If they tell you they're choosing someone else or sticking with the status quo, you obviously want to understand why.

The best way to get back into a deal is if there is some fundamental disconnect between you and the customer. Once you've discovered this, be assertive as to why they should reconsider.

Escalate if you need to with an email along the lines of:

Dear X,

We were recently informed that you were going in another direction regarding your purchase of X platform. We dug into this and it turns out that there was a significant misunderstanding as to [e.g., the level of integration involved].

Your team's misinformed assumptions resulted in a much longer and costlier integration than it actually would be, and I take responsibil-

---

61   Brightcove and Ooyala were bitter competitors. Ironically, Ooyala bought Videoplaza. It was weird but fun to compete against friends and former colleagues.

ity for that confusion. We believe in long-term, mutually beneficial relationships and have believed our two companies are a great fit [list out the reasons why]. It would be a shame to miss out on working together due to a misunderstanding. I'd respectfully request you to reconsider the decision based on this new data and would be happy to discuss further at your convenience.

If that doesn't work, understand the real reasons why the customer didn't choose you. This seems obvious but oftentimes a rep wants to move on and will say they lost the deal on price. This is a cop-out. Don't fall for it. Losing a deal on price actually means that the customer didn't perceive the value in your product so you shouldn't have pursued it, or you did a bad job of conveying the value. Sometimes the customer has other reasons that they feel uncomfortable sharing with you, like not liking or trusting your team, but they cite price as a graceful way to bow out.

Keep probing until you get to the real reasons. Customers can be reticent with feedback. The most frustrating is when procurement stonewalls you or your counterpart ghosts you altogether. Escalate to the highest level you have access to or even cold email the CEO. Try something like:

Dear X,

I am CEO of Y. We offer a platform to [fill in the blanks]. My team has been engaged with your [name the team] in a process to evaluate [CRM platforms] for your company. We were recently notified that we weren't selected to move forward. Naturally this was a disappointment as we believed we had a strong mutual value proposition.

However, despite multiple tries, we have not been able to get any feedback behind the decision. I can certainly respect your team's decision but getting insight behind this will help us greatly. We have invested a lot of time together and I would personally appreciate it if you could facilitate reaching proper closure on this.

Coming in a close second on a deal is usually the worst outcome.

Often overlooked, enterprise sales processes are expensive to run, easily costing upwards of tens of thousands of dollars when factoring in time spent by the sales rep, sales engineering, and other functions to support complex deals, not to mention the opportunity costs on top. So, you had better make every one count. It's better to qualify out or get to a quick no than have a long, drawn-out no during which you've spent a lot of time on the deal. The only time it's worth being a close second is if whoever won the deal stumbles and the customer has to scramble for an alternative. Hopefully you've been hanging around the rim.

Hang around the rim on strategic accounts.

In basketball, hanging around the rim is when a shot has been made and you then make the effort to go to the basket, timing your jump to grab the rebound and score in case of a loose shot. This is a good metaphor for strategic accounts that are hard to crack. Perhaps they're working with an incumbent. Perhaps you've been blocked by a gatekeeper and are having a hard time getting in. No matter.

If they're that important, you need to hang around the rim. That means continuing to provide updates and having regular touch-points. Sharing content and periodic updates is a thoughtful way to do this. Then, one day, you'll spot the loose ball. Perhaps the incumbent is failing. Or the gatekeeper has moved on. Jump on the ball and stuff it in the hoop.

Move on.

Losing deals is painful, especially when you got outsold or made mistakes that could have swung it in your favor. Sometimes you did everything right and you still didn't get chosen or had to qualify out at the eleventh hour. There was a deal at Ooyala where the competition came in and essentially proposed a JV involving equity with the sports publisher we were pitching. There's no way we could compete with that and so we qualified out. We'd worked hard on the deal and had it forecasted so it hurt. Don't sweat these. You can do everything right and still not win the deal. It's important for you and your team to learn and then move on. Confidence is everything.

Ring the bell.

Celebrate when deals close. The bigger the deal, the bigger the celebration. Getting enterprise deals over the line is no small feat and involves a lot of teamwork. Give your team the recognition that is due and find ways to celebrate from pats on the back to team dinners or trips. Thank the customer for the deal and consider other gestures to cement the experience—for instance a thoughtful gift or a personalized cake.

ASSESSING YOUR REPEATABLE SALES MACHINE

Sales is highly transparent so it should be easy to know when you've moved beyond founder selling. Beyond having a team generating and closing their own deals, metrics on lead generation, pipeline growth, quota attainment, time to rep productivity, and pipeline predictability are all KPIs that you've built a repeatable sales machine. Ultimately, these are proxies for predictability:

- Do you have the playbook and processes to recruit and onboard reps to productivity? It matters not if it's weeks or months in high-velocity motions or several quarters in big-ticket enterprise motions. What matters is if you have the pattern recognition to do this repeatedly.
- How well can you predict the output of your sales machine based on inputs such as marketing spend and number of quota-carrying heads? This will inform the story for your subsequent fundraising rounds.
- How accurately can you call the bookings you'll hit at the start of a quarter? You'll be hard-pressed to get to 100 percent, especially in "lumpy" businesses, but 80 percent is sufficient. If you can call your bookings attainment for the next quarter plus or minus 20 percent, you've built a repeatable sales machine.

There's one more indicator: AE and CSM morale.

Operating in the trenches, AEs and CSMs are closest to your customers and the competition and therefore the canary in the coal mine. Demoralized reps indicate larger problems with product readiness, your beachhead market, or your value proposition. It's one thing for a rep to have a bad week of meetings, quite another if your reps lack confidence across the board.

On the other hand, having your field team waking up every day with a spring in their step is a very good sign indeed. It's time to scale your organization. And yourself. We'll cover that next in Part 3.

PART 3

SCALE YOUR HUMAN CAPITAL

Sometime in early 2007, Elisabeth, my boss at Brightcove, pulled me aside. "At some point, Rags, you're going to have to start carrying a quota." That was hard to swallow. I'd done our first and largest deals but, as a business "athlete" wearing multiple hats, I enjoyed playing in other areas. It couldn't last. I'd have to give some Legos away and specialize.[62]

Brightcove was on a tear, having tripled revenue the past two years. We were also feeling the growing pains, like unclear roles and responsibilities from having simultaneously pursued multiple products and business models. Luckily, Jeremy Allaire and Bob Mason, the Brightcove founders, had hired seasoned executives like Elisabeth earlier than most startups, and they provided the leadership to drive focus and steer us through our period of hypergrowth.[63] We blew past Ten all the way to IPO in 2012.

Scaling human capital comprises the third leg of the stool to go from One to Ten. It's also the hardest one to nail. Whether it's executing reorganizations, implementing new processes, or transitioning early employees, scaling human capital can be messy, emotionally fraught, and filled with what we euphemistically call "growing pains." Growth feels good. But the pain part of it is real too. Not everyone may be along for the next stage in your journey. Not everyone will be up to "give away their Legos" and take a narrower but deeper role.

You will need to scale yourself on this journey and get out of

---

62   One of First Round's most popular articles, an interview of Molly Graham: "'Give Away Your Legos' and Other Commandments for Scaling Startups," First Round Review, accessed June 13, 2021, https://firstround.com/review/give-away-your-legos-and-other-commandments-for-scaling-startups. Well worth a read.

63   Including Tareef Kawaf, now President of RStudio; Adam Berrey, marketing extraordinaire and future startup CEO; and Andy Feinberg, who went on to become CEO of Brightcove before forming Argon Ventures with Bob.

your comfort zone. You'll no longer be the expert at everything. You'll need to trust your team with key responsibilities. Scary? Maybe. But you can do this. You must.

Scaling human capital starts with ensuring alignment so people know how their work fits into the bigger picture. That means having a strategic plan and then implementing an operating cadence to ensure you're executing the plan. We'll then delve into organizational design and how to recruit and get the best out of your people. We'll finish with the scariest and loneliest part of all: scaling yourself.

❖❖❖

CHAPTER 12

ALIGN YOUR VECTORS

Do we "play offense" and attack the US or defend our home turf in Europe? What about Asia and Latin America where we have some customers and pipeline? Should we invest in the nascent but growing opportunity in programmatic video? Or do we go horizontal in adtech and add capabilities such as display and mobile ads? Or should we go up the video stack into linear TV?

Videoplaza faced these strategic questions in 2014 with a set of initiatives behind each one. Each strategy on its own made great sense. Put them together with the consequent set of activities, however, and we were spinning. We had AEs chasing leads in Latin America, BD execs negotiating partnerships for programmatic advertising, and product managers scoping out banner ads to add to our platform. Our vectors weren't aligned.

Founder and CTO of HubSpot, Dharmesh Shah, wrote a memorable blog post, "What Elon Musk Taught Me about Growing a Business."[64] He relates how he attended an intimate dinner during which he asked Elon for his advice on growing a busi-

---

64   Dharmesh Shah, "What Elon Musk Taught Me about Growing a Business," thinkgrowth.org, October 16, 2017, https://thinkgrowth.org/what-elon-musk-taught-me-about-growing-a-business-c2c173f5bff3.

ness. Elon's response: **"Every person in your company is a vector. Your progress is determined by the sum of all vectors."**

That did not make for a pretty picture at Videoplaza. We needed a strategic framework to define what we were betting on, and a vocabulary that would align the vectors. As importantly, we needed a not-to-do list to make it crystal clear what we were willing to trade off.

So, that's what we did. We commenced a strategy planning process that served to reinforce our mission and vision and clarify the strategies to pursue these. The strategic plan naturally informed the operating plan and budget for the subsequent year. It worked so well that Ooyala, our eventual acquirer, adopted a version of it for their own use.

You will want to do the same. This may sound complicated, but it need not be. All you're doing is connecting your mission to the key initiatives to focus on in a given time period. Ultimately, it empowers your staff, enabling them to tie their work to your company's mission.

A FRAMEWORK FOR STRATEGIC PLANNING

There are many ways to do a strategic plan. Choose a framework that resonates for you and stick with it. Two of the best I've seen are Lenny Rachitsky's[65] and Marc Benioff's V2MOM framework used by Salesforce.com.[66] You can also use a consultant to facilitate your planning, who will likely have their own framework.

---

65 Lenny Rachitsky and Nels Gilbreth, "The Secret to a Great Planning Process—Lessons from Airbnb and Eventbrite," First Round Review, accessed June 13, 2021, https://firstround.com/review/the-secret-to-a-great-planning-process-lessons-from-airbnb-and-eventbrite.

66 Marc Benioff, "Create Strategic Company Alignment with a V2MOM," Salesforce, May 1, 2020, https://www.salesforce.com/blog/how-to-create-alignment-within-your-company.

Regardless of which framework you use, the output should clearly lay out your mission, an objective, and a cohesive set of strategies toward achieving this in a given time period. Create a not-to-do list explicitly articulating what you won't do. Adapt the following simple strategy and budget planning process to your own needs:

- Invite the management team and other key stakeholders, for instance chief architects, product manager, and finance. It's important that they actively contribute to the work product so as to be invested in the outputs.
- Revisit and recommit to the company's mission and vision. As the founder, you are uniquely positioned to remind people why they're there, why they've come together to do something bigger than themselves. This should be done at every all-hands meeting for that matter.
- Agree on the present state comprising a SWOT[67] analysis, market trends, and the competitive landscape. Assigning this to nonmanagement stakeholders will force others to take stock and provide a window as to how they view the business.
- Agree on what won't change in the next ten years.

---

67   Strengths, weaknesses, opportunities, and threats.

From Jeff Bezos:

> I very frequently get the question: "What's going to change in the next ten years?" And that is a very interesting question; it's a very common one. I almost never get the question: "What's not going to change in the next ten years?" And I submit to you that that second question is actually the more important of the two—because you can build a business strategy around the things that are stable in time. [...] In our retail business, we know that customers want low prices, and I know that's going to be true ten years from now. They want fast delivery; they want vast selection. It's impossible to imagine a future ten years from now where a customer comes up and says, "Jeff, I love Amazon; I just wish the prices were a little higher," [or] "I love Amazon; I just wish you'd deliver a little more slowly." Impossible. [...] When you have something that you know is true, even over the long term, you can afford to put a lot of energy into it.[68]

- Agree on the future state in two to three years. Sketch out paths to get to the future state. There are various ways to do this, but they all boil down to your product road map, your go-to-market, financing, and talent. Assign homework to people or teams in the form of straw-man proposals, discussion documents, or business plans for each initiative that can then be discussed by the wider group. Use the following exercises to bring each initiative to life:
  - *Write the press release.* Ask the team to write a press release imagining success in the endeavor.
  - *Do a premortem.* Assume that you've failed in the future. Describe the failure and the factors that led to it.
- Determine a measurable objective for the next year that ties to the future state and reflects your mission. For example,

---

68 Jillian D'Onfro, "Jeff Bezos' brilliant advice for anyone running a business," Business Insider, January 31, 2015, https://www.businessinsider.com/jeff-bezos-brilliant-advice-for-anyone-running-a-business-2015-1.

take Dvinci. If their mission is to accelerate the transition to renewable energy, their objective in the next year might be to triple the number of solar installations facilitated by their platform.

- Define three major initiatives that will achieve this objective. These should be big enough to make or break your year and encompass your product, go-to-market, and geo strategies.
- Model what it will take to execute on these initiatives and how it impacts your financial plan. Iterate based on input from your cross-functional teams and constraints you impose in terms of burn and resources. This is where real trade-offs get made, where horse-trading is done.
- Output and pressure test three scenarios with your team and your board. Understand the upside levers and downside risks to each one. Bring these scenarios to your board along with your recommendation.
- Assign your functional owners to do functional plans. In fact, they should already have been doing this in parallel, having been involved in the process. For instance, if one of the major initiatives is to increase sales velocity, what are the set of initiatives for the go-to-market team to pursue and what will they need in terms of head count and budget to achieve this outcome?
- Your board will weigh in and more iteration may be needed before approval. Tweak the functional plans as needed and cascade communications to the rest of your org.

STRATEGY PLANNING CADENCE

Develop a stage-appropriate cadence to your planning. Too frequent and you risk whipsawing the organization. Too seldom and you'll miss trends in a dynamic market. In general, twice a year or every quarter will be where you land. Here's what we had at Videoplaza:[69]

Midyear	Q3	Q4	Early Q1
Conduct offsite:	Synthesize work stream inputs into strategic plan	Iterate on budget	All hands kickoff:
Articulate strategic questions		Gain board approval	Present plan for year
Determine work streams	Commence budgeting process		

MENTAL MODELS FOR STRATEGIC DECISION-MAKING

As you and your team explore various strategic options, you will face a number of hard choices. Use the following heuristics to guide your strategic decisions.

Let confidence drive your investment decisions.

How should you determine how fast to go, how much to invest, how hot to burn? Revenues are a lagging indicator. They reflect the processes you ran in the past based on the state of your product back then. Bookings and ARR are better but often don't tell the full picture. Confidence is the best leading indicator. The confidence you and your management team have in your product and business should drive your level of investment. But be honest with yourselves, too. Beware vanity metrics or hubris that lead to the wrong decisions.

The US market is by far the biggest, and most crowded, advertising market in the world. A frequent topic at board meetings, the US was a potentially huge growth lever. But while we made some forays, we didn't go all in. While we didn't say this explic-

---

69 Our fiscal year was based on the calendar year.

itly, we lacked the confidence in our platform, both the tech debt and lack of table stakes features relative to the competition. This was the right call. We instead focused on keeping and growing our existing customers and expanding in Asia, all of which was part of the strategic rationale for our acquisition by Telstra/Ooyala.

You can be confident in your road map but also decide to wait before doubling down. Perhaps you're early in your market and it will be a few years before the market truly breaks your way. That's fine; bide your time in the meanwhile.

That's exactly the case for one of my portfolio companies in the cloud analytics space. They are in a market rife with legacy workflows and platforms and a hesitancy to adopt the cloud. This is yielding linear but not exponential growth from the early adopters that do adopt. Now is not the time to put the pedal to the metal. The market isn't quite there. They will grow for the next few years and be well-positioned when the market inflects.

Use inflection points to drive your future state planning.

Startup valuations don't increase linearly. Rather, inflection points drive step changes in valuation and unlock access to capital. Think through your inflection points and use these to drive your strategic planning, and your fundraising strategy for that matter.

Remember Asylon, the drone-in-a-box platform providing aerial security as a service for its customers. They broke through in 2020 with a number of big customer wins and robust bookings growth. Yet, they decided not to go for a larger fundraise until after they hit their next inflection point. Currently, due to

FAA regulations, their drone operations require a pilot on-site to provide oversight. Their next inflection point will be when they get their first FAA waiver to operate the drone remotely at a site and radically improve their margins. This will unlock more sites with existing customers, more net new customers, and funding.

Where can you double down?

Larry Cheng of Volition Capital recounts a piece of wisdom from Jeff Bezos, who asked of a company, "Is there anything big or small that is working better than you expected? Is there anywhere we could double down?"[70] As Larry explains it, "Jeff's point was that we spend a lot of time focusing on what's not working in board meetings…and not enough time focusing on what is surpassing expectations and how we can 'double down' on those areas. Oftentimes the key levers in businesses are found in little things that are really outperforming whether by intention or not…either adjacent enough or small enough that they wouldn't make a board presentation or be an obvious discussion point because they're just seedlings that need to be watered." Do you have seedlings to be watered? Where should you double down?

Embrace constraints.

Constraints—your runway, market size, market dynamics— drive clarity. As Rylan Hamilton put it, "We didn't have the luxury of a lot of funding, but it forced us to rapidly iterate in the field and be really scrappy from the beginning. Building beta units by hand, doing upgrades at 11:30 p.m. on a Saturday

---

70   Larry Cheng, "How Can We Double Down?" May 19, 2009, https://larrycheng.com/2009/05/19/how-can-we-double-down.

night, dealing with electronic discharge issues on our robots…it really felt like we were building the airplane while flying it. I'm not sure we would have been able to get to the same outcome had we raised a monster $70 million round early on."

Assess your growth initiatives on the matrix below.

	Existing Markets	New Markets
New Product	**Harder**	**Hardest – Only for big pivots**
Existing Product	**Easiest**	**Harder**

How much growth is possible selling existing products to existing customers and verticals? If there's plenty of growth there, stop thinking about new markets and new products and focus your planning on the bottom left box. At Videoplaza, we had slowing growth from our core and so had to choose between new products and new markets. And avoid going diagonal unless you're doing a big pivot.

Drown puppies.

I heard this memorable (and awful!) phrase early on in Brightcove and it has stuck ever since. Puppies refers to (cute) well-intentioned projects that have some justification but never make it onto the critical path. Yet, they seem to never go away either, often because someone is tied to them for emotional reasons. And we all know that caring for puppies, however low maintenance, requires resources and energy.

Puppies are distractions from your critical path. Learn how to recognize puppies. And drown them. Easier said than done, right? Mercilessly killing projects that others are emotionally invested in can impact morale. It's even worse if you have puppy projects with customers and revenues. How to handle these? It's all about providing context.

Start with your mission and vision. Whether it's to employees or customers, remind them why your company exists, how that's driving the strategy and key priorities, and show how the puppy project falls outside of this. Be firm about the decision and try to avoid hedging qualifications like "we can't proceed at this time." That indicates that you might in the future and people may be tempted to keep working on it on the side. Get personally involved to deliver the message to any impacted customers and go the extra mile so you don't leave them high and dry, for instance by giving them plenty of notice or helping them find alternate solutions.

Minimize regret.

Choose the path most likely to cause the least regret. Let's say you're faced with selling the company to a buyer for $50 million versus "going for it" by raising more funding to go for more growth and a much larger outcome. There would of course be many factors at play but, on the face of it, think through each option and potential scenarios therein. Let's say you sold for $50 million and then saw a competitor go it alone and end up selling for $500 million. How would it make you feel to have missed out on so much upside? Then, think about not taking the offer in favor of going it alone and, worst case, having a competitor outgun you and selling for pennies on the dollar. How much would you regret not having sold? These thought experiments can surface your appetite for risk and upside, which is what often underpins strategic decisions.

Once you have a strategic plan, it's important to communicate it crisply and frequently. The more employees know what's on and off strategy, the more autonomy they have to make their own decisions instead of having to run them up the chain. The more empowered they are, the more creative and productive they will be. It's important to clearly communicate what's off strategy, the puppies that have been drowned, or risk these projects showing up again begging for attention.

Develop a concise presentation and share via 1:1s, team settings, and all-hands settings. It will feel repetitive to you. Good. Err on the side of overcommunicating. It feels repetitive only because you've been living and breathing it.

The litmus test you should follow is whether everyone in the company is able to tie their work to their team's goals, and in turn, tie those to the company's strategy and overall mission.

Strategic alignment is great but it's nothing without operational excellence. We'll cover that next.

CHAPTER 13

ACHIEVE OPERATIONAL EXCELLENCE

I recently started working with a founder in the One-to-Ten phase. In one of his first emails to me, he wrote:

We're at the point where we're ready to keep scaling, but I've never quite been able to implement an effective management/operational system. Specifically, we've never had all of these pieces working at once:

- Setting performance expectations and KPIs for teams
- Setting goals quarterly across the company
- Communicating and aligning around the goals
- Tracking and reporting progress
- Getting feedback and improving

Without these elements, we aren't really able to generate accountability and alignment around our business goals. We're ending up doing a lot of cultural and alignment firefighting versus executing smoothly.

Does this sound familiar? First you need a strategy, which we covered in the prior chapter. You then need a management system to execute on the strategy and ensure the right balance between autonomy and alignment. We'll cover that now.

ACHIEVE ALIGNMENT VIA OBJECTIVES AND A CADENCE
OBJECTIVES AND KEY RESULTS

Translate your plan into objectives and key results. The OKR framework, famously espoused by Intel and then Google, is effective to bring transparency and accountability across functions. It also enables autonomy because each function or individual determines how to achieve the key results that will impact their objectives. You'll find a lot of material on adopting OKRs[71] so I won't go deep, but do bear in mind:

- KRs should truly be key results, not actions.
  - *Good*: "A successful 1.0 product launch as measured by at least three beta customers, at least thirty inbound leads, and at least one piece of favorable coverage."
  - *Less Good*: "A successful 1.0 product launch as measured by speaking to ten customers, creating three inbound marketing campaigns, and writing a press release."
- **Use OKRs to drive stretch goals.** I prefer the Google approach to setting OKRs such that 70 to 80 percent achievement will be meaningful and 100 percent achievement would be game-changing. As Perdoo puts it, "Group Key Results should reflect a big change, something that, if you achieve 70% to 80% of your target, the rest of your orga-

---

71   First Round Review has a good article on how to make these work so you might start here: "How to Make OKRs Actually Work at Your Startup," First Round Review, accessed June 13, 2021, https://firstround.com/review/How-to-Make-OKRs-Actually-Work-at-Your-Startup.

nization will notice. Make them tough. If they're easy to achieve they're not challenging enough."[72]

Whatever system you use to drive operational alignment and accountability, it's important to commit to it. OKRs fail when there isn't consistency, when there isn't buy-in from the top, or when they don't reflect a new strategy. That means reviewing OKRs at your exec and all-hands meetings.

DEVELOP AN OPERATIONAL CADENCE

The legendary David Sacks writes about the operating cadence he used at Yammer and PayPal.[73] It's targeted at enterprise SaaS companies but can be adapted to your own business. The principles include first, time-synching sales with finance and marketing with product with an offset of half a quarter between the two. Next, conduct tentpole product launch events each quarter that galvanize the product, engineering, and marketing orgs around a certain date.

We did versions of this at Videoplaza and Brightcove, although the half-quarter offset is genius. Setting up a cadence for the year, whether it's sales kickoffs, board meetings, or external events, will mean lines in the sand that act as forcing functions for your strategic initiatives.

RUN GREAT MEETINGS

People complain about meetings because they are too often ineffective. Then they complain when they're not invited to

---

72 "The Ultimate OKR Guide," Perdoo, accessed June 13, 2021, https://www.perdoo.com/okr-guide.

73 David Sacks, "The Cadence: How to Operate a SaaS Startup," Craft Ventures, July 1, 2020, https://medium.com/craft-ventures/the-cadence-how-to-operate-a-saas-startup-436aa8099e8.

meetings and don't have their voice heard. Meetings are necessary. They also add up. Just think of all the 1:1s, team standups, program reviews, all hands in place. Ineffective meetings destroy value in insidious ways. A bad one-hour executive staff meeting costs you $556,[74] not to mention the opportunity costs of having a good meeting in, say, not making a decision. Now, add that up over the course of a year and across your company and it can be a big number.

Meetings should have agendas, the right people in the room, and accountability. At one company, we saw a video from EOS on how to run a "Level 10" meeting[75] and we immediately put it into place, raising the level of our meetings. The highlights:

- **Small Talk:** Everyone should be present at least five minutes before the start, engaging in small talk, catching up on the weekend.[76]
- **Punctuality:** Start the meeting on time.
- **Good News (five minutes):** Everyone gives one bit of good news, either professional or personal. This breaks the ice and sets the tone for the rest of the meeting.
- **Reporting Mode:** Build out an issues list to discuss later as you review the following around the room (five minutes per item):
  - *Scorecard*: Go through KPIs. Are these on track?
  - *Rock Review*: Review large priorities for the quarter.
  - *Customer / Employees* : Good and bad news, one sentence headlines.

---

74   Back of envelope: five execs at average of $200k/year working an average of 1800 hours/year = $555 plus.

75   EOS Worldwide, "Effective Meetings: Level 10 Meeting for Entrepreneurial Leadership Teams," April 25, 2014, https://www.youtube.com/watch?v=HmV6_fH5NkU.

76   This is harder, more awkward to do on Zoom calls but these platforms will improve to better enable informal chitchat.

- **Review To-do List (five minutes):** Review last week's outstanding to-dos. Most should be dropping off each week or else there may be an accountability problem.
- "Identify Discuss Solve" Mode (sixty minutes):
  - Prioritize issues list by importance.
  - Identify the actual issue.
  - Discuss the issue openly and honestly; determine options.
  - Solve, noting any action items on the to-do list.
  - Repeat for the next issue on the list until you run out of time.
- Conclude Meeting (five minutes):
  - Recap the to-do list and owners.
  - Discuss any messages that need to be cascaded down through org.
  - Rate meeting on a scale of one to ten. Probe the reasons behind anyone giving a score of seven or less.
  - End meeting on time.

MENTAL MODELS FOR OPERATING EXCELLENCE

While there are many ways to successfully execute your strategy, the following management principles have served me well over the years.

Focus on the critical path.

Do you and your team know what must be nailed to hit your plan? This is your critical path. Write these down and stress test them. Are certain items really on that critical path, or are they nice-to-have distractions? Do you have the right level of resource and focus on these critical-path items?

Identify the points of friction on this path and systematically work to eliminate those. Clear the plates of those responsible for the work. Everything else is noise. Or puppies. Everyone should understand the critical path and where their work fits into it.

Operate at Minimum Viable Parallel.

As an entrepreneur, many of your biggest, most challenging decisions will be around resource allocation and whether to proceed in serial or parallel. You can't only operate serially—you have to have at least some parallel initiatives. For instance, you can't stop your business operations altogether to go fundraise. But the more you do in parallel, the more you dilute resources, especially your own bandwidth. So, you have to determine what you absolutely must do right now and what you can sequence until later. This decision-making doesn't go away, and you'll need to calibrate constantly. I call this "Minimum Viable Parallel." What are the few things you really need to nail to get to the next level?

It's tempting to do more in parallel, to spin up concurrent teams and initiatives. I've succumbed to this temptation many a time. Each project on its own seems benign and doable with the considerable bandwidth of you and your talented management team. Beware! Be honest about what you and your team can truly take on at any given time. And then be ruthless about what really needs to be prioritized now and what can be sequenced until later. So, what do you currently have in flight? Should any of these be sequenced until later? Are you really at Minimum Viable Parallel?

Don't innovate unnecessarily.

There are certain processes, platforms, and functions where

innovation won't move the needle. For instance, avoid a drawn-out process to select a CRM and just choose a tool that you and your sales reps are familiar with.[77] The marginal increase in productivity that you'll get from selecting and integrating the perfect CRM is easily outweighed by the cost and distraction of going through the process in the first place. You can swap CRM systems in the Ten-to-X phase.

Don't overengineer platforms.

I've seen engineering teams spend weeks debating the merits of a certain tool or worse, adding tasks to their sprints to optimize a tool, rather than picking something that's good enough and getting on with it. Be vigilant on teams overengineering their tools and platforms in areas where it just won't move the needle.

Institute a culture of documentation and retrospection.

Amazon is famous for banning slide presentations in favor of written memoranda. Stripe values writing so much that they have their own publishing imprint. Half-baked, lazy ideas can be obfuscated by bullet points in a PowerPoint. But there's no hiding in a six-page memo. As remote work becomes more prevalent during and post-COVID19-pandemic, a culture of documentation, and of writing, will become ever more important. Document important concepts such as your operating principles, how decisions get made, and how products get shipped.[78]

Hopefully you have a culture where people are willing to hold

---

77 Salesforce is the most powerful yet complex. Many startups can do fine with HubSpot, Pipedrive, or even Airtable.

78 You should already have documented your sales playbook when creating your repeatable sales machine.

themselves accountable. Constructive retrospection, regardless of the outcome, creates positive feedback loops. Celebrate what went well and recognize those who did well. Honestly acknowledge what didn't go well and how to avoid this in the future. Then share the retrospectives with everyone. We had a culture of this at Videoplaza that served us well.

Audit your "decision-making inbox" to diagnose your business operations.

This technique involves inspecting the topics that flow through to you for decisions or where you need to get more heavily involved. For instance, as GM of EMEA at Ooyala, I had outside field reps asking me about approving rate card discounts on their deals. These were garden-variety deals and they'd had guidance as to what was acceptable and when to get their direct manager involved. That meant something was broken either in how we communicated our pricing policies or what the level of sales management below me understood, and was easily rectified. On the other hand, I was glad to get requests to interview or help close promising candidates—recruiting and training is a high-leverage activity for any exec.

You also want to understand what doesn't make it to your inbox to make sure the filter isn't too tight. Sit in on team meetings from time to time or conduct skip-level meetings to understand what's happening on the ground.

Celebrate heroes while rooting out the need for heroism.

Heroism abounds during early startup years. The engineer that pulls all-nighters for a week to make a committed ship date. The professional services team that gives up their summer holiday to hit a customer deadline. The field engineering team that, MacGyver-style, pulls a victory from the jaws of defeat at a deployment gone wrong.

Recognize these heroes who have gone above and beyond the call of duty. At the same time, be clear-eyed as to what drove the need for the heroism in the first place. Was it an unrealistic deadline, broken processes, ineffective communication protocols, underperforming employees, not enough resources? Requiring heroism for every deployment or product launch won't scale. Heroism should proportionally decrease as you go from One to Ten.

Strive for "loosely coupled" tight alignment when managing people.

I recently heard this phrase from the first Netflix CEO, and it immediately resonated. "What they really want is freedom and responsibility. They want to be loosely coupled but tightly aligned."[79] This goes to that balance between alignment and autonomy. You want your team to know what they're trying to achieve, internalize how their work impacts the greater mission, and have the freedom to determine how to achieve those outcomes.

Focus on the inputs and processes. The outcomes will follow.

Last, focus on the inputs, the primitives. Were you happy with how a sales rep conducted a meeting? Did the hardware team prepare a thoughtful program review? Are you having productive discussions at your weekly management team meeting?

79 Andy Weissman, "You'll Figure It Out," *Maximum serendipity* (blog), January 18, 2021, http://blog.aweissman.com/2021/01/youll-figure-it-out_18.html.

Ensuring quality inputs and processes that you control will, over time, lead to good outcomes.

Scaling human capital requires strategic alignment and operational excellence and, well, humans. It means getting the most out of your people and having them in the right roles. We'll cover this in the next two chapters.

CHAPTER 14

LEVERAGE YOUR HUMAN CAPITAL

"It's the people...maybe my best advice is, after even a couple million in revenue...if you're still doing a VP function, stop. Go hire the person...After $10 million, all that matters is your VPs. Nothing matters but your executives."[80]

—JASON LEMKIN, FOUNDER OF SAASTR, ECHOSIGN

Trite but true, your people are your most important assets. Your company's success is inextricably linked to your human capital and how you best leverage it. I'll start with culture and go on to cover hiring and developing talent.

"Culture eats strategy for breakfast."

—PETER DRUCKER

---

80 "'Godfather of SaaS' Jason Lemkin on 2020's cloud software boom, public CEO mindsets, how Zoom conquered the competition & more," *This Week in Startups*, video, December 2, 2020, https://thisweekinstartups.com/e1147-godfather-of-saas-jason-lemkin-on-2020s-cloud-software-boom-public-ceo-mindsets-how-zoom-conquered-the-competition-more-rising-stars-of-saas-8.

Culture can be a force multiplier to get you from One to Ten, or it can destroy value. I've seen companies with cultures that felt like the real-life version of *Silicon Valley* the TV show. It didn't end well.

Videoplaza was the opposite. We were an underdog, undercapitalized in the smaller European market. And yet our culture was something special. We recruited A-level talent[81] attracted to our ethos of humility, excellence, and having fun. All was well.

Then, in 2014, our US competitor, FreeWheel, finally attacked Europe. They hired a managing director who engaged a recruiting firm that called all of my commercial team offering similar roles at 20+ percent pay increases. Not a single person jumped ship. That's the power of culture.

Culture is what you do, not what you say.

Be thoughtful about what type of culture and values you aspire to. And then live them. Ben Horowitz puts it best in the title of his book *What You Do Is Who You Are*. It's that simple. You can communicate the type of culture you wish to foster but it will be for naught if you don't actually walk the walk.

Your startup is not a family.

Considering your startup a family is tempting, especially when going from Zero to One, when you're working closely with your co-founders and early employees. But startups are not families. Family implies that someone can never leave, that people have the same titles and roles. Instead, the mental model should be

---

81   As I write this, my former direct reports are CEO of a VC-backed startup in Sweden, GM EMEA for a Series D Valley-based marketing tech company, and CRO at a European SaaS startup.

that of a team, a band, a community, or even a platoon. This will make it easier to shuffle responsibilities or to part ways with people.

The team analogy is most accessible to me since I'm an avid athlete. You can be considered a team and still be asked to sit games out or even leave the squad. It doesn't take away from your prior contributions, but there's also the recognition that the team expects everyone to hold their own, or even that some types of players may not gel with the playing style of the team at that moment in time and thus need to be benched.

B2B enterprise startups should take care of employees, customers, and shareholders in that order.

I first heard this from Ramesh Srinivasan[82] and it immediately resonated. Happy employees lead to happy customers, which in turn lead to happy shareholders. It's that simple. You don't need to be irresponsible or extravagant, but take care of your employees and make sure they're recognized. At one Series B company, I was disappointed to find out that one of their employees was traveling coach class from Boston to Asia and then expected to hit the ground running in a high-pressure environment. There wasn't an official travel policy in place at the time; rather the understanding was to use one's judgment. To their credit, the employee and his boss were frugal—an important trait in startups. And yet, don't be penny-wise and pound-foolish when taking care of your employees.

---

82 Currently CEO of publicly traded Agilysys, he was my boss at Ooyala. I learned a ton during his short, difficult tenure there.

HIRE GREAT PEOPLE

People make a disproportionate impact on your venture's trajectory. And yet, the way we hire seems weird. Just imagine, we make offers to people we expect to work with for years based on how they perform over several hours of those staged, contrived activities we call interviews. How weird is that? More importantly, how do you up your recruiting game?

Hire for attitude, aptitude, and experience in that order.

Optimize for attitude and aptitude over experience unless it's a highly specialized technical role or a high-pressure commercial role like VP of sales. Experience counts equally for these types of roles. Having the right attitude is paramount to success in early-stage startups where change is the one constant. Do they show an ability to adapt? Are they coachable? How do they take feedback and what's an example of feedback they took on board? Have they changed their mind on something? These are all good questions to probe on attitude.

In terms of aptitude, I look for evidence of the ability to learn. I'll ask how someone learns and to tell me about one recent thing they've learned that they're excited about.

As for experience, I ask candidates to point to the one accomplishment of theirs that would point to success in the role in question. I want to understand how they perceive the role, what success would look like, and how they tie this back to their track record.

Reference early, not late.

Employers tend to take candidate references at the tail end of a process just prior to giving an offer. This doesn't make sense. At that point, it becomes a box-checking exercise. Even worse, the temptation is to hear what you want to hear since you're already invested in the candidate and don't want to start over. Flip the model and take references toward the beginning of a process, especially for executive roles.

Try before you buy.

Look for ways to ascertain what it would be like to work with someone outside of the interview setting. I have product, sales, and marketing candidates give a presentation either on our business or on a product they're familiar with. The former is harder as they won't have the context but it's also more of an opportunity for the candidate to shine. Communication skills manifest more naturally in presentation settings. Do they think quickly on their feet in response to pointed questions or a changed agenda? How do you feel about this person representing you and your company in a meeting when you might not be there?

If presentations aren't as important, what other joint exercises could you do for each party to get a feel for what it'd be like to work with each other? Perhaps you could invite an engineer to sit through a design review. Or go through a fake business model with a finance candidate. I'm currently evaluating an opportunity where the founder invited me to a private Slack channel to be able to bounce thoughts off each other. It's been a natural way to test chemistry and how we work through problems.

While it won't be possible for all candidates, you can also get to know key hires via some sort of engagement, such as an advisor, a consultant, or a board member, before diving in. This enables both parties to get to know each other without having to fully commit right away. I've used this approach for my last four roles and only made one mistake.

Raise the average.

Every candidate you hire should raise the average caliber of the team they'll be joining. Amazon famously uses this strategy by explicitly having a "bar raiser" from another department interview candidates to ensure that they will increase the quality of that team.

Hire VPs at the early stages of growth.

Many founders mistakenly hire executives too late after achieving product–market fit. They then experience rapid growth and have to scramble to recruit them while the organizational debt piles up. Hire functional leaders who can help you scale up earlier than you think. Elad Gil nails it when he writes: "Hiring bona fide executives well in advance before things break is the difference between a sudden ongoing meltdown at your company versus not. Many founders wait to hire executives 'when we have enough scale to support them,' instead of viewing the executives as crucial to supporting future scale. The thought process is inappropriately inverted. Executives exist to help you scale and run the company, not the other way around."

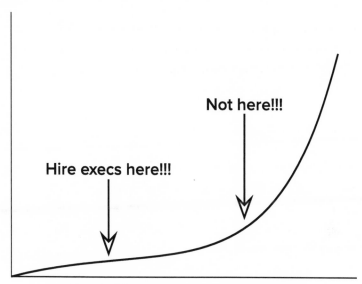

Days Since Product-Market Fit

And here's Jason Lemkin[83]:

> The #1 hiring mistake founders make after $1 million ARR:
>
> A manager instead of a VP of Marketing
>
> A manager instead of a VP of Product
>
> ...
>
> A product manager for now, not a VP of Engineering
>
> First, the junior hire costs **more**...They don't pay for themselves...A true VP is accretive.

---

83   Jason Lemkin (@jasonlk), "The #1 hiring mistake founders make after $1M ARR" Twitter, https://twitter. com/jasonlk/status/1355632676540039169?lang=en.

Second, you get burned out. A true VP takes 80–100% of the function off your plate. Compare that to a junior hire who just helps you implement stuff. Do not confuse the two.

Find the budget for the few extra dollars for a true VP. It pays off very, very fast. A true VP is a profit center.

Well said. At Brightcove, we greatly benefited from having seasoned VPs in place who could build their functions out, which contributed to our initial years of hypergrowth.

Always be recruiting.

Fill your talent pipeline even if you're not currently hiring for a role. Maybe you're impressed by the account manager from one of your vendors. Could she be a future hire for you? Or that director of engineering from a partner who may be looking for their next career move in six months. Don't be afraid to drop hints either: "I've really been enjoying working with you. You seem happy where you are now, but if you ever start thinking about what's next, we'd love to have a conversation."

Recruiting talent can be a long game. I left Brightcove in 2012, after a seven-year run in online video. I'd been speaking to Sorosh Tavakoli, who was looking to build out his team, including his board. I told him I'd be glad to be part of the board, but I was done with video and so there was no way I'd join full-time. Fast-forward ten months, and a lot of conversations, and I'd joined full-time as chief commercial officer.

Recruit those you can't hire to be on your board or as an advisor.

Ben Rubenstein is another rock star. A serial entrepreneur, he founded Opcity in 2015 and sold it three years later to Realtor.com, where he is now CRO, for $210 million. Dvinci has a very similar model to Opcity, but there's no way Walid would be able to recruit Ben. So, he did the next best thing by convincing Ben to join the Dvinci board.

Cultivate a well-functioning board.

Your board will look different at Ten than it did at One. Your investors will be represented on your board, but consider the rest of the board's makeup. Bias toward a smaller, tighter-knit board. Avoid the large board with lots of observers at this stage of your company. Large boards beget performative dynamics and prevent substantive discussion. Have at least one independent director seat and use it wisely. Perhaps there's someone who got you to where you are, but it makes sense to rotate them out. You want someone independent yet founder-friendly. Someone who has the bandwidth to be involved and add value.

Use your board and advisors to close candidates.

Trotted out at the right moment, your board and advisors can be the wild card in closing outstanding candidates. Do not hesitate to use them to close candidates, even ones who are a couple of levels down. Recruiting is very much part of the remit of any board member or advisor.

DEVELOP GREAT PEOPLE

Technical founders with engineering mindsets tend to undervalue the impact that good people management can have. Poor people management saps morale and drags companies down. You'll find lots of blog posts and entire books written about how to manage people. I won't rehash those here, but the following concepts have particular resonance for me and for the founders I've worked with.

Grow "stem cells."

Deep tech startups often find a thin pool of talent with direct relevant experience. This is natural. You're breaking new ground and, by definition, there won't be many companies doing the same thing that you can poach from. This was a common issue we encountered at Videoplaza—there just weren't that many candidates experienced in ad server integrations. What's one to do?

Grow the talent. We recruited less experienced, but talented, candidates willing to learn. The obvious trade-off was the steeper learning curve and longer time to get productive. But the strategy paid off where we developed awesome talent that made a big impact, were relatively cheaper than more seasoned hires, and stayed longer. That's what my friend and serial entrepreneur Brian O'Kelley[84] did at AppNexus. AppNexus would go to top universities and hire talent based on attitude and aptitude for their global services team. They'd rotate these hires through various customer success or implementation roles until they landed in the ideal team.[85] They called these "stem cells." Brian said, "We didn't know what they'd develop into at the time, just that they had a lot of potential." The trade-off with this approach is time. It takes time to train junior talent. But

---

84 I was one of his first beta publishers when he was CTO of Right Media inventing programmatic advertising, which sold to Yahoo for $680 million. He went on to found AppNexus and sold it to Verizon for between $1.6 and $2 billion. He's now working on his third startup, Waybridge.

85 This is not a new innovation—large, old-school companies like IBM have rotation programs—less so at scaleups.

the payoffs in terms of culture, retention, and bang for the buck can be significant.

Over-index on training as you grow.

Training is one of the highest-leverage activities and yet is often an afterthought until companies get much bigger. Too often, hiring managers expect new hires to get up to speed via osmosis. Sure, that approach works. But investing in better training upfront has a compounding effect. New hires get productive quicker, product ships earlier, sales close more, and you have a virtuous cycle.

Most growth-stage startups, where first-time managers abound, underinvest in manager training. While there may be plenty of documentation on company culture and playbooks, there is scant little on how to manage people. Many first-time managers muddle through, learning hard lessons along the way that can be costly. It needn't be this way.

At one of my prior companies, an inexperienced engineering manager put one of his new direct reports under a PIP[86] with no warning. The report was shell-shocked, having recently been promoted by their prior manager. As you can imagine, we had to spend lots of cycles dealing with this. We could have avoided this with some basic manager training. That prodded our HR to implement a manager training program.[87] Well-received by everyone, it even served as a recruiting tool for those aspiring to be managers one day.

---

86 Performance improvement plan—these are formal plans when someone is underperforming and must show improvement or else be terminated.

87 There are third-party consultants that do this. I also think this is something a VC can offer portfolio companies as a shared service.

Last, training is also about motivating new hires with the company vision and mission and where they fit in. Put yourself in the shoes of the fiftieth person you hire. Why should they be fired up to come in to work every day, to put in those extra hours? Your responsibility as founder is to inculcate the new hires with your mission and vision.

Hire people ops sooner than you think.

People ops is a rebranding of human resources (HR) to get beyond negative perceptions of HR as a cost center mainly administering payroll and benefits and ensuring that the company doesn't get sued. Whatever you call it, it's a strategic function and should report to the CEO.

Founders tend to wait too long to get a proper people ops leader in. Don't. Start off with a director-level hire who can be your business partner. Having the right person in charge of people can provide you huge leverage from hiring rock star candidates to improving employee engagement and retention. Better to pay a few months extra salary in hiring someone too early than wait too long and lose out on great candidates or employees.

At Videoplaza, I spent more time with Hanna, our awesome Head of People Ops, than I did with any of my direct reports. She certainly was responsible for the administration aspects of the role but, beyond that, she was a crucial business partner in helping me manage my team, whether it was sensing flight risks, coaching underperformers, or recruiting. I trusted her intuition and we built a team with low attrition and high performers that went on to take bigger roles at our acquirer and at other companies.

Hire slow, fire fast.

This is hard to do. Almost everyone will tell you that they regret not having parted ways sooner with someone who wasn't working out. We all hear this advice, nod our heads, and then make the same mistake, myself very much included. We are human, after all. Having formal thirty-, sixty-, and ninety-day check-ins with new hires helps to ensure that expectations are aligned and nip any problems from the start or else provide each party with a regular forum to surface discontent.

Employee attrition, voluntary or not, is on you.

Hold yourself accountable when you do have to part ways with someone. Did you not set them up for success? Did your urgency in having to fill the seat cause you to look past certain flags during the interview process? By that same token, employees who leave on their own accord are also a reflection of you and your company. Be honest with yourself about the reasons they left and what you can learn from it. For some employees, there's a natural end to their run based on where they are in their career and in their lives, and the stage of the company. This was me in late 2011 when it felt right to leave Brightcove.

It's the other instances that are more painful. The ones where a valued employee left and you felt like they had a lot more to contribute, a lot of room to advance. Yet they lost faith, in the mission, in the company, in you. Look in the mirror and acknowledge what you did to enable this. It will do you good.

In general, we underestimate what our reports are capable of.

Ramesh Srinivasan, my former boss at Ooyala, would always

say this, exhorting us to get out of the way of the people we managed. His philosophy is to give people high expectations, empower them to act, and trust them to get the job done. This works well when your vectors are aligned and the feedback loop is in place to know what's working and drive accountability.

Finding and developing great talent is half of the human capital puzzle. The other half involves placing them in the right positions. We'll cover that next.

CHAPTER 15

SCALE YOUR ORGANIZATION

Scaling your organization means putting the right people in the right places. It also means leveling up. You and your management team will need to operate at a different level, whether it's taking on a wider span of control, more direct reports, or more responsibility. As you grow, you will likely need to do at least one reorganization. I've seen many reorganizations. The ones that went well involved great stakeholder management, crisp communications, and a swift execution. Those that didn't were emotionally fraught and full of drama, where decisions would linger and people would spin, leading to instability, infighting, and attrition. It comes down to clarity of decisions, roles, and responsibilities, and tying the changes to the overall mission.

ORGANIZATIONAL DESIGN

"When you create an organization chart you are creating your product—the seams in the organization get reflected in the product; the depth of feature work gets reflected in resource allocation;

the coordination across job functions gets reflected by the leaders you choose."[88]

—STEVEN SINOFSKY

Organizational designs can be based on function, geography, business unit, or some combination thereof. There is no perfect organizational design, just the one that is best for your specific context and what you're optimizing. Your head of people should be intimately involved in thinking through and executing any reorg. Use the following principles when planning reorganizations:

- Clearly define why you need to do a reorg and what you're optimizing for. For example, "We need a focused, cross-functional team to develop our next-gen product." Also, be clear on what you're willing to trade off.
- Bias toward a flatter, more horizontal organization. Having fewer hops between you and those "at the coalface" will mean greater customer empathy. You do not want to be far removed from customers ever, let alone at such an early stage.
- Bias toward "two pizza" teams that have a singular mission and the resources to achieve it. Jeff Bezos famously keeps teams working on new products small enough that two pizzas will feed them. Small, focused teams get lots done. On the other hand, you are baking in complexity if your teams will need to work with others to achieve their goal.
- Avoid a matrixed organization. Matrixed organizations, with solid lines and dotted lines, are for big companies. Having a matrixed org at an early stage probably means that you're trying to take too much on at once. I've been guilty of this

---

88   Steven Sinofsky, "Functional versus Unit Organizations," Learning By Shipping, December 3, 2016, https://medium.learningbyshipping.com/functional-versus-unit-organizations-6b82bfbaa57.

at one of my companies where one engineering team had to serve two masters. Even though we had one engineer per project, it still led to complexity, distraction, and lower velocity.

- Write down the jobs to be done, and then determine which functional teams can take these on. It's easier to understand what needs to be done than get caught up in labels and titles.
- Design your organization as if you were starting from a blank sheet today. That's the ideal state. Now, compare it to your current state. For instance, maybe you'd have one VP of engineering in your ideal state but it's not possible today given the players involved. You can then decide whether to keep the status quo or make a change.
- Avoid frequent, wholesale reorganizations. Plan for any reorganization to have at least a twelve-month life or you risk whipsawing your team to distraction.
- Coincide organizational changes with company inflection points like shipping a product, completing a fundraising, or landing a big customer. These make it easier to explain the "why now" to employees.
- Optimize reporting lines for communication. For instance, you might have pre-sales and post-sales in the same group at first since they'll be sharing resources and will work closely together with customers.
    - Observe informal communication pathways. We've all seen courtyards with paved paths in carefully drawn lines and then the shortcuts that people take across the grass. These eventually get paved over. Where does that exist in your organization? That may be an indication to put those teams together.
- Be sure to get stakeholder input as you're considering the organization change. Even if you don't follow their input, it will make it much easier to roll out as they will appreciate

having their opinions solicited and not having decisions rammed down their throat.

- Limit spans of control to six to eight direct reports. It's very tough to effectively manage more than eight direct reports.
- Don't let organization changes linger. Changes in reporting line, span of control, responsibility, and title are a big deal for your managers and their teams. These discussions will be distracting, so be efficient in terms of both the planning and the execution.
- Overcommunicate when you roll out a reorganization. First, speak directly to the managers and team members who may be affected, following the same script on why the changes and what that means for them. Then, roll it out at an all-hands meeting with the same script. You never want people affected by an organizational change to hear it first in a group setting.

Don't overengineer your functions.

Avoid overengineering functions and creating silos prematurely. I remember the first trip we made to our acquirer's offices after our acquisition. We spent the first day with each functional team presenting to their counterparts.

It was intimidating sitting through our new colleagues' slickly designed presentations chock-full of impressive-sounding data and unfamiliar lingo. Our scrappy presentations paled by comparison.

Turns out, in the ensuing year, our team had the best churn and hit the highest percentage of plan across the company. Why? We had the benefit of being scrappy and not being bogged down by process or constrained by silos. If one of our French customers had a problem, the Paris team was on it, whether someone was in sales, CSM, or support. Contrast that with our American counterparts with their overengineered organization who had to go up the chain to have resources allocated to a ticket or to be able to travel to a customer.

Prioritize hires based on leverage.

As Ben Horowitz says, "You either apply pressure or you feel pressure." Ask yourself, does your management team provide you leverage? If you're spending too much time with someone on areas that really should be their responsibility, you're not getting the leverage you need. For example, you've hired someone in finance but still find yourself in the spreadsheet weeds to model your business. A great way to gauge leverage is how you'd feel if this person were to do an important meeting—an investor due diligence call, a customer pitch, a product kickoff, a company all-hands—without you being present.

Your finance function should be strategic.

A strong finance function is a must to go from One to Ten. Finance is perceived as simply counting beans and ensuring that employees and vendors get paid. That's accounting. Finance is strategic and drives planning and fundraising. Founders often start off with fractional CFOs and outsourced finance. It's fine to do this but you'll want to hire someone full-time to lead this function around the time of your Series A. What to look for in such a role?

- Someone adept at finance, planning, and analysis (FP&A) who can truly partner with you, sales, and marketing on business model, pricing, margins, and structuring deals.

- Someone you can fundraise with. You should be comfortable having this person do an investor due diligence call without you.
- A good communicator who can present internally while also being comfortable in boardroom settings.
- Last, you want someone who's not afraid to challenge you or your team. Finance is both an enabler and part of a system of checks and balances to ensure good governance. The last thing you want is for finance to roll over when challenged by sales.

Retire organizational debt.

In Part 1, we covered technical debt and the need to pay it down as you go from One to Ten. The same concept applies when company building. Just as you've optimized for speed to market on the product, you've done the same with your company and incurred organizational debt along the way. Perhaps you gave someone a title they don't qualify for or paid over the odds to get a key hire on board, or hired a product manager with the expectation that they'll lead the group when it's clear they don't have those chops. Maybe you have some early advisors or investors that aren't adding value and, in fact, are more of a distraction. This is all organizational debt.

Determine where you may have organizational debt and stack rank in order of urgency. Most of the time, this is around org design—titles, roles, and responsibilities that will hamper growth. Early jack-of-all-trades employees can be the cause of organizational debt if they can't or aren't willing to specialize. I wore a variety of hats during the early days of Brightcove, dabbling in BD, sales, marketing, and the like. I remember when my manager had the conversation with me about me needing to carry a quota. It only then dawned on me that the organization had grown and I'd have to give up my Legos or move on.[89]

The most expensive organizational debt, however, tends to revolve around co-founders and their roles.

FIND FOUNDER–ORGANIZATION FIT

I remember the uncomfortable silence. The squirming in seats. It was a cold winter night and I was presenting at Harvard's Launch Lab X about lessons learned from twenty years in tech to a room full of young startups. I had just remarked that, more often than not as a startup scales, one of the founders emerges as the clear leader, while their co-founders take other roles or else exit the business. The audience wasn't expecting to hear this during their honeymoon phase of working together.

And yet, not every founder can scale with the needs of the business. This is not something that new founding teams pay attention to, but it can be the most pernicious organizational debt to tackle. Perhaps the founder was brilliant during the Zero-to-One phase but isn't interested in scaling beyond that. Technical founders often take on managerial responsibilities and then realize it's not for them. They're happier staying as an individual contributor and becoming an expert in their discipline.

These are delicate and often difficult conversations to have. But they must be had, or else painful founder breakups can threaten the value you've painstakingly created. Investors can help provoke the conversation but will be reticent to get too involved

---

89   I gritted my teeth and became a bag-carrying salesman. It was awesome. I learned how to sell.

unless it is becoming toxic to the whole company. No VC today wants to have a reputation for meddling with founding teams and breaking up the band.

So have a regular, honest dialogue with your co-founders and align expectations:

- Reestablish the "why" behind your coming together in the first place. Have those reasons changed or is there a different context? Perhaps your co-founder has a family and needs a certain type of income that your startup isn't able to provide. That happened to one of my startups recently where one founder bought the other one out.
- Commit to at least a yearly check-in with each other in which you take stock and discuss roles for the upcoming year. It only works if each person honestly reflects as to whether they're really the best person to occupy their current role for the next year.
- Determine the best role for each founder accordingly. Sometimes it means a transition out of the operations of the business, either to the board or out of the company altogether.

Founder transitions should be driven by the founder themselves. The worst is when the founder doesn't recognize their limitations or holds on to a role too long. The end result is the same—taking another role or being nudged out of the business. But they could have avoided a lot of angst and stress by being proactive about it. Don't be that founder.

CHAPTER 16

SCALE YOURSELF

Leveling up your organization isn't easy. It can mean hurt feelings and disgruntled early employees. The best way to affect this change is to level yourself up. Where do you need to up your game or learn new skills? Perhaps it's public speaking or learning how to hire. You will need to challenge yourself out of your comfort zone to go from One to Ten.

Start by understanding how you're viewed by those around you. Push for candid and constructive feedback of your strengths and weaknesses. Your head of people or a board member can help get anonymized 360-degree feedback if you don't think you'll get the right level of candor through direct conversations. The more honest you are about your superpowers and how you can best add value, the better you'll be able to support the company's growth and continue to be excited about your personal impact.

According to Wikipedia, the Peter Principle is a concept, developed by Laurence Peter, "which observes that people in a hierarchy tend to rise to their 'level of incompetence.'" The Peter Plateau, then, is the point at which people get stuck at their level of incompetence. What is your plateau today and how can you break through? Like one founder I know, perhaps you are an ace engineer, but you need to hone your storytelling and marketing skills to really take the company, and yourself, to the next level. He is already rising to this challenge. How about you?

Improve your storytelling.

We are the stories that we tell. To ourselves. To one another. As a founder, you will need to excel at telling stories. In fact, having come this far, you've already been telling stories to recruit your co-founders and early employees, to close your first investors and customers.

As you grow, your stories will need to evolve. That founding story of hatching your company on a napkin won't resonate for your next set of investors, customers, or employees. Your stories need to be stage-appropriate while keeping your mission and vision at their core.

I took a chance on a young company and a first-time founder based on one slide. It was 2011. We were in a café in Covent Garden in London. Sorosh Tavakoli, the ebullient founder of Videoplaza, whipped out his laptop and walked me through their deck. He had me at the second slide.

Evolution of TV Ad Spend

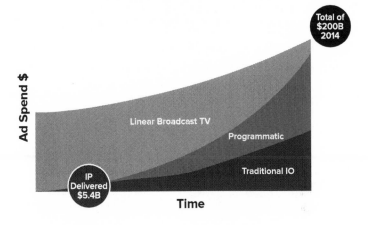

No data sources given. No geography. Not even a timeline for the shift.

And yet! I immediately grokked the inexorable shift toward digital video, that the TV ad market would follow suit, and that I wanted to be a part of this historic shift. We ribbed Sorosh about that slide but boy was it effective.

As we grew bigger, as the market matured and got more sophisticated, the story would also need to evolve to one of being the dominant video monetization platform in Europe, to being a mission-critical system of record to optimize video revenues… you get the picture.

What's your story now? Is it still founding-story led and does it need updating based on your company and market maturity? And what's the one slide that will do the selling?

Confidence is key. Pay attention to what might be holding you back.

"Sorry guys, I'm just not feeling it," said Sorosh, slowly shaking his head. We'd been working on a business plan for a new product. We'd spent weeks on the market analysis, customer trends, and financial model. But all this data still couldn't convince Sorosh to go for it. Rationally, he was there. Emotionally, something was holding him back.

Sorosh is one of the most intuition-centric, emotion-driven entrepreneurs I've ever met. It was bemusing and, at times, frustrating to my highly structured, engineering-centric brain. I remember reading the first update when I joined his board, sprinkled with the words "I feel." I remember shaking my head—I'd never read such emotion in business memoranda.

I learned so much from Sorosh. Turns out, he had to "feel it" to be able to pitch. We all do, right? The thing is, we as humans trust people who project confidence but not too much of it. We distrust those who come across as too confident and blustery. We also don't want to buy from those who don't appear confident. Would you buy from someone with a downward gaze, sweat pouring from their forehead?

That's Sorosh when he lacks confidence in what he's saying. I've been in meetings when that was the case, and it wasn't pretty. But when Sorosh feels it, he's unstoppable. Charismatic and passionate, you can't help but want to work with him, to want him to succeed. We had to get him to this place.

We dug in with Sorosh. He was imagining himself in a room full of agency executives and didn't feel confident in telling our story. We worked through expected questions and objections. This iterative process honed our message and value proposition. We knew we were there when Sorosh felt confident to be able to take it to the world. Months later, we launched the new product with a multimillion-dollar run rate that ultimately helped us sell Videoplaza.

Engineers like to make data-driven decisions. I did too. Then I met Sorosh Tavakoli. He made decisions based on gut. I learned to do the same and it changed me as a leader. Sorosh is on one end of that spectrum, but you should still listen to your gut. Why does something not sit well with you? Your emotions are data points too.

Diagnose your culture and your contribution to it.

Act like an anthropologist and catalog the behaviors you observe. Now, tie these back to your own. Videoplaza's founders were college friends and would hug when seeing each other. This practice filtered down to everyone else. What behaviors have you observed that you want to encourage, and which ones are not okay? What part do you have in those? Commit to modeling the right behavior.

You are complicit if you accommodate bad behavior.

At one prior company, we had a talented but highly strung executive. He was prone to meltdowns. His behavior risked creating a toxic environment. We gave him candid and constructive feedback and tried various ways to address this behavior to no avail. Having him around was sending the wrong message to the rest of the employees, that bad behavior might be tolerated as long as one was productive. So, we had to part ways despite his considerable contributions. It's one thing to coach underperforming employees to help them level up, quite another to tolerate bad behavior.

Write a user guide.

I first heard about this concept on First Round Review.[90] User guides describe how you best operate and communicate, and how others can best work with you. Instead of having people work out your management style and your idiosyncrasies over time, save your team the hassle and just write these down and make it available to those you'll work closely with. This can be as a Google Doc, wiki/Notion page, or whichever format you prefer, as long as it's easily accessible to those who need it.

Optimize for your superpowers.

Think back over the past year. When did you have the most fun, the most fulfillment? Where did you have the most impact? When are you most energized? What drains you of energy? Optimize around your superpowers and delegate the rest. That's where you can have the most impact. For instance, you may be getting bogged down by the numerous decisions you need to make in a week, especially in areas like finance that bog you down, or to just put a road trip together. You could instead be spending that energy on product design, which would really move the needle. Perhaps it's time to hire a fractional CFO or a chief of staff, about which we'll discuss later.

Audit your calendar and your inbox.

Understand where you're spending your time and mental energy. Forensically going through your calendar and inbox and allocating time spent to various buckets will give empirical data that you can match to what the allocation ought to be. The

---

90   "The Indispensable Document for the Modern Manager," First Round Review, accessed June 13, 2021, https://firstround.com/review/the-indispensable-document-for-the-modern-manager.

most mission-critical items ought to be getting 50 to 80 percent of your attention.

Last fall, I was catching up with the founder of a high-growth marketplace startup, where I'm an investor. He described how they'd achieved product–market fit for the supply side, which was now more predictable, but that building for the buy side would really unlock their path to $100 million ARR. As we spoke, it seemed that he was relying too much on someone he'd hired in and not spending enough time on it himself, being bogged down by the vagaries of running a business. My recommendation was for him to delegate as much as possible and dive into the buy side with the new hire.

Use the points of a compass to calibrate how you're spending your time (a useful framework that my coach once used on me). North represents those you report to, or your board and investors if you're the CEO. East is customers and prospects. South is employees or recruits. West represents your peers in the company, or the broader market if you're CEO, such as partners, press, and competitors.

You will need to over-index in one quadrant based on your business context. For instance, the blue line in the following diagram might be you when you're fundraising, and the red line post-fundraising when you're hiring and going to market. Whatever it is, be deliberate about it and let your team know.

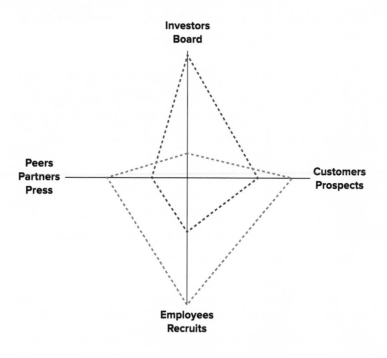

How are you allocating your time across these quadrants and are there discrepancies? Now make sure your calendar actually reflects your decision. For the calendar does not lie.

Use the Bezos 2x2 matrix for decision-making and how you spend your time.

Pete Flint of NFX recounted a conversation with Jeff Bezos about how he decides to rethink a decision: "He said, 'If this is a decision that's highly consequential and irreversible, then I'm going to keep myself open to rethinking as long as possible because once I've made the investment, I can't undo it and the stakes are really high. But if it's reversible or if I think it's inconsequential, then I'm going to act quickly, and over time,

I know I'll have lots of opportunities to rethink in reaction to the feedback that I get in response to the data."[91]

I try not to sweat decisions that are reversible. Some decisions may go wrong, but as long as the risk is manageable and I'm able to cut the cord on any decision, the speed and clarity of making the decision itself is liberating and leads to faster learning.

Get a coach.

I bridled when Sorosh once suggested that I use the coach he was using. What did I need a coach for? I should be able to do my job on my own. Needing a coach was a sign of weakness. Wrong.

If the top athletes and tech CEOs in the world benefit from coaches, you can too. You may already have advisors who have been helpful sounding boards. While an advisor may be useful for certain connections or domain experience, a coach will focus on helping you be the best version of yourself. As such, a coach goes one level further and gets more deeply engaged, say, sitting in on your management team meetings, helping with your 360-performance review, and having a regular 1:1 with you.

Consider hiring a chief of staff.

Chiefs of staff give CEOs leverage. They report to you and, while the scope will vary based on the context, they can help with admin, filling gaps, keeping your schedule, and holding you accountable. That's essentially what I did at my first job in tech at Live365. First Round Review has a good overview of the CoS

---

91   Pete Flint, "Anti-Patterns of 10x Thinkers," NFX, accessed June 13, 2021, https://www.nfx.com/post/anti-patterns-of-10x-thinking.

role: "This is a position scoped for the CEO, and it has elements of both an executive assistant and a COO. Like an EA, a Chief of Staff works only for the CEO and doesn't have direct reports... Like a COO, a CoS works on strategic and critical items, working with employees as well as customers and board members. To be very clear: while the CoS makes many important decisions and has strong leadership skills, this is a service role. The job is to make [the CEO] a superhero."[92]

What would your successor do?

Dave Girouard, the founder of Upstart, recounts a brilliant mental model that he uses to level himself up.[93] "Another mental exercise I've invested in is thinking about what would happen if tomorrow my board got together and fired me...they found the very best CEO in the world...And if they bring her in and she starts at Upstart—what would she do differently than what I'm doing? I think about that for a while, and then I tell myself, 'Why the hell aren't you doing those things?'"

I've since used this thought experiment. A company I was advising was in the middle of a pivot, but they weren't letting go of the legacy business. Instead of helping them on both fronts, I asked myself what another advisor would do, and it was immediately obvious. I challenged the founder to choose one path or the other and go all in on it. Which he did.

Send regular, written updates.

---

92 "Why You Need Two Chiefs in the Executive Office," First Round Review, accessed June 13, 2021, https://firstround.com/review/why-you-need-two-chiefs-in-the-executive-office.

93 "Fresh Off IPO, Upstart's CEO Shares Why the Startup Isn't a Typical Success Story," First Round Review, accessed June 13, 2021, https://firstround.com/review/fresh-off-ipo-upstarts-ceo-shares-why-the-startup-isnt-a-typical-success-story.

The process of compiling regular, written updates is of itself helpful in forcing you to rise above the fray and see the forest for the trees. The discipline and reflection required may be causal in better outcomes. Jason Calacanis, the journalist and entrepreneur turned prolific angel investor, requires his start-ups to send monthly updates. He once wrote, "If your startup isn't sending you monthly updates, it's going out of business." Mathilde Collin, the founder of Front, takes it a step further, articulating the three emails every founder needs to send:

- A weekly revenue update to the whole company
- A weekly update to her direct reports with her priorities and what's top of mind
- A monthly investor update with KPIs, key events (both good and bad), and asks

Mathilde puts it well: "Since I've started angel investing, I feel even more strongly about this practice. After a founder sends me two or three update emails, I can immediately get a sense for whether or not that company will succeed...Some send an email and then you don't hear from them again for four months. Others use different formats or metrics every time. Or they say that revenue is the top priority in one meeting and then say they're focusing on engagement and redesigning the app in the next. That's not an update, that's an excuse. If revenue isn't where it needs to be, admit that you have an issue to your investors, your team, and above all yourself so you can start getting back on track."

Take care of yourself.

Startups are not for the faint of heart. The grinding, the stress, can take its toll. But it really is a marathon with a series of sprints in between. Don't be the hero who doesn't take any vacations for years and then eventually burns out. Be sure to have the right outlets to take your mind off work and let steam out. For me, this involves playing sports, meditating, cooking, and hanging with family and friends. It doesn't matter what it is, be disciplined about making time for self-care. And take vacations where you can properly switch off. You'll come back refreshed and able to approach problems from a different perspective. You won't be doing anyone any favors by burning yourself out.

Let go.

Finally, learn to let go. Easier said than done for most founders. But at some point, you will need to trust your VP of engineering to manage and scale those developers, to make way for your head of product to own the road map, to let your CFO lead the preparations for the next fundraise. Ed Sim of Boldstart Ventures tweeted it well: "Learning to let go for founders who are used to doing everything is one of the hardest things to do, especially for first-timers. But until you learn that you are the blocker to scale + repeatability, you will limit your upside. The trick is sequencing."

CONCLUSION

As I write this, I'm working with a handful of startups on the journey from One to Ten.

Dvinci is farthest along and may well be past Ten by the time this book comes out. For Walid Halty, it's mainly about scaling their human capital. Having bootstrapped Dvinci for so long, Walid took most activities on his shoulders. They are now in hypergrowth mode and he recognizes that won't scale, that he has to delegate more, build out an executive team, and mature their organization. But I'm not worried about Walid. He's got this.

Damon Henry and Asylon are also well on their way. Their drone-in-a-box platform is in production with missions being flown 24/7/365, logging thousands of hours each month. He also will need to scale his human capital to achieve their big unlock—proving to the FAA that they don't need a pilot on-site.

Abhishek Jha of Elucidata is focused on building a repeatable sales engine. He will need to prove that others can sell to get to the next level. So far, so good based on some recent hires.

And then there's Butlr, the property tech startup, founded by Honghao Deng and Jiani Wang, that I recently joined as president. We also are on the journey from One to Ten and will soon be tested across all three dimensions of product readiness, repeatable sales, and organization scaling. Wish us luck.

What about you? What do you need to nail to unlock the next level of growth? What will you do differently?

And how will you know when you've done it? When your customers are clamoring for more. When your sales team's hitting quota with predictability. When you realize an important piece of work—landing a big deal, a successful design review, a QBR—happened without your involvement, and you were happy with the outcome. When you're feeling good about the story to tell for your growth round. At that point you'll know that you've gone from One to Ten.

What next? Ten to X, of course. Multiple products. International expansion. M&A. Teams of teams. Growth financing. The list goes on.

You'll need to push yourself out of your comfort zone again. To do things that don't scale for new products and initiatives. But you can do this. You've done it already.

There are few startups that make it to Ten. Celebrate what you've accomplished. Your work isn't done but you're well on your way. Drop me a line so I can cheer you on.

Onward and upward.

ACKNOWLEDGMENTS

This book started on a lark. The COVID-19 pandemic had set in, I'd transitioned out of Humatics, and Scribe Media happened to put on a virtual book school. Thanks to them and their community for their tutelage and support along the way, and to my mother and my wife, Tatiana, for encouraging me to go for it.

Thanks to those whom I quoted or whose stories I told in the book, including Abhishek Jha, Walid Halty, Damon Henry, James Richards, Amy Villeneuve, Brian O'Kelley, Jonathan Tushman, Celine Kimberly, Sonci Honnoll, Rylan Hamilton, Carlos Nouche, Kash Razzaghi, Tareef Kawaf, and those who can't be named.

Thanks to my beta readers for providing encouragement and constructive feedback: Branick Weix, Quantum Wei, and especially Jeff Orkin and Jeff Whatcott.

Thanks to the founders and managers that I've worked for. I've learned much from each and every one of you, including Alex Sanford, Jeremy Allaire, Elisabeth Bentel Carpenter, Andy Feinberg, Vanessa Wade, David Mendels, Ben Regensburger, Sorosh

Tavakoli, Jay Fulcher, Ramesh Srinivasan, Charlotte Yarkoni, David Mindell, Gary Cohen, and Ramesh Raskar.

I'm grateful to Honghao Deng for having me along for the Butlr journey, and to Matt Rhodes Kropf of Tectonic Ventures and MIT Sloan for having connected us. Let's do this.

Thanks to the countless entrepreneurs that I've advised or invested in over the years. You are an inspiration.

Thanks to the university early-stage venture ecosystem for all that you do, notably Jinane Abounadi of MIT Sandbox, the folks at the Princeton Entrepreneurship Council, David Chang of Babson Summer Catalyst, and Thara Pillai of Harvard's Launch Lab X.

Thanks to Adam Valkin, Bob Mason, and Adam Berrey for your guidance and generosity with connections when I moved to Boston from London.

Thanks to the TBD Angels founders for creating one of the most engaged tech communities out there.

Thanks to the folks at Hyperplane, especially Vivjan Myrto, Naimish Patel, John Murphy, Jack Klinck, Samara Gordon, and Blake Billiet, for having me on the team and showing me the ropes.

Thanks to Ed Zschau for opening my eyes to a career in tech entrepreneurship, and for being a steadfast mentor, helping guide me through dicey times early in my career. Thanks to Frank Moss for his mentorship in more recent years.

Thanks to the folks at Lioncrest/Scribe, including Tara Long for an awesome cover design, Skyler White for helping me nail the title, Mariano Paniello for patiently creating and reworking the graphics, and Miles Rote for guiding me on all things book marketing. Special thanks to my editors Hal Clifford and Mckenna Bailey for your support and tough love, and especially to my publishing manager, Neddie Ann Underwood, for your energy, enthusiasm, and organizational superpowers that kept the project on track and got this book across the line.

Thanks to my family and friends for all the moral support, not least my brother, Ro Gupta (himself a tech entrepreneur on quite the journey with Carmera), my sister-in-law, Ki Mae Heussner, and especially my mother and father for asking about the book's progress and nudging me along when it was slow going.

Thanks to my daughter, Nina "Mishti," for delivering me baked goods with a smile as I toiled away on the book in the home office, and to my son, Milo "Babu," for keeping my spirits up with his letter writing and card making.

Thanks most of all to my wife, Tatiana. I couldn't have done it without you. You are the best.

Made in the USA
Middletown, DE
07 October 2021